D1499184

CONCILIUM

THEOLOGY IN THE AGE OF RENEWAL

CONCILIUM

CONCILIUM/VOL. 40

SCRIPTURE

THE BREAKING
OF BREAD

edited by PIERRE BENOIT, O.P.
ROLAND E. MURPHY, O.CARM.
BASTIAAN VAN IERSEL, S.M.M.

VOLUME 40

CONCILIUM
theology in the age of renewal

PAULIST PRESS
NEW YORK, N.Y. / GLEN ROCK, N.J.

CONTENTS

PREFACE

Pierre Benoit, O.P./*Jerusalem*
Roland E. Murphy, O.Carm./*Washington, D. C.*
Bastiaan van Iersel, S.M.M./*Nijmegen, Netherlands*

In his yearning for the infinite, man makes an effort to encounter the supreme, perfect being whom he senses above him. He calls this being, God, and he would like to know him, to make contact with him, to enter into a living relationship with him. He longs for an existential encounter with this being so that he might enjoy his "presence".

This is the encounter for which so many of our contemporaries pine, often without realizing it. But instead, their questions often renounce this possibility: "Does this being really exist? Must we not speak rather of God's tragic absence?" The death-of-God theology is the fashion of the day.

But is God really dead? Are we not talking about a caricature of God when we speak in these terms? Is atheism really a denial of God, or is it rather the rejection of a false God fashioned by man himself?

In biblical revelation God manifests himself as the Living One. It is a concrete, existential manifestation in history. God chooses to overcome the resistance of sin and the cavil of reason by encountering man in the totality of his existence. The biblical God comes to men and dwells with them. Man is both body and soul, and God chooses to encounter man's soul through his body. This physical, sensible, corporeal aspect of the God-man encounter is the theme of this present volume of *Concilium*.

1

To "visit" sinful man and to restore to him the divine presence which he had lost, the God of the Old Testament chose to meet man in the realm of the senses, in his very flesh. The age-old rites of the shared meal and communion are adopted to provide life-giving contact through nourishment.

The People of God, starving in the desert, were nourished by the manna. Its deliverance from captivity in Egypt is recapitulated in a meal, and the ritual repetition of this meal communicates the power of this miraculous deliverance to succeeding generations. By eating the bitter herbs, the unleavened bread and the paschal lamb, each succeeding generation of Israelites relives the saving presence of God which brought them into the promised land.

This sacred meal, rich in memories and promises, is taken over by Jesus; into it he will infuse the rich treasure of his new, definitive deliverance. It is the enslavement of sin, not captivity in Egypt, from which he delivers man. And he does this by sacrificing himself, the spotless lamb, offering his life for the salvation of the world. Any and all who participate in this meal, who eat his flesh and drink his blood, share in his sacrifice and receive its fruits. God's presence, which had been lost, is restored to them in a love that pardons and in the most concrete way possible. The soul is brought to life while the body is nourished.

The early Christians repeated the actions of their Master. In Jerusalem, and later in all the localities where they settled down, they brought him back into their midst by repeating his words and his actions. Through the "breaking of bread", the presence of their crucified and risen Lord is rendered concrete to them once again. Every time they do this, they are more deeply involved in the new covenant which he sealed with his blood. They "proclaim the death of the Lord until he comes". They are inserted into the "body of Christ", of which they are the members. The water of wisdom and the manna of the desert have become for them the flesh and blood of the Lord, communicating to them the life of the Spirit.

This fundamental rite—real presence in sacrifice and communion—is re-presented every day in our Mass. The liturgical rubrics have undergone change and development, but the underlying reality is the same. To celebrate Mass is to "bless" (*eulogia*), to "give thanks" (*eucharistia*). It is the living and final expression of what had been typified in the Old Testament, and the "type" has become reality; shadow has given way to light-giving substance. The spiritual food which nourishes the new life is no longer a symbolic prefigurement. It is now a present reality: the body of the risen Lord who communicates his life to us.

The transformation of bread and wine into the Lord's body and blood is not a change of substance that remains locked within the confines of this world. It is the ancient world of creation catapulting into the new world of a second creation. It is an entry into the eschatological world through the elements of this present world.

In the body of Christ, which he touches, tastes and assimilates, the communicant encounters the new humanity as a whole. He also encounters the new cosmos, of which the risen Christ is the head.

The eucharist nourishes the Church. Through the sacramental order, of which the Church is the center, God touches and renews the world. He makes himself present to the universe. The incarnation achieves its full effect. God offers his presence to men, to all men, in the most intimate way imaginable.

Let us hope that man will be capable of responding to God's invitation: "Behold, I stand at the door and knock; if anyone hears my voice and opens the door, I will come in to him and eat with him, and he with me" (Apoc 3, 20).

PART I
ARTICLES

Pierre Grelot/*Paris, France*

God's Presence and Man's Communion with Him in the Old Testament

The question of religion is existential in nature. It is not a question of having ideas about God or of talking about him; it is a matter of entering into a concrete relationship with him. Man wants to experience God's presence somehow, through signs which manifest it unambiguously; and he wants to live in communion with God on a quasi-experiential level.

God's revelation in the two testaments identifies the obstacle which complicates the solution of the religious question. Although man is created in the image of God and continues to bear this imprint, his existence unfolds under the mark of sin from the very beginning (cf. Gen. 3). That is why God's presence is not directly perceptible to man in a creation that should manifest it with crystal clarity; that is also why communion with God cannot be a sense experience within the scope of man's efforts.

For man, God is both present and absent, both near and far away. He is present and near as the creator, since man is dependent on God for his very existence. He is absent and far away insofar as man looks for him from within the framework of his own sinful condition. Here we have an antinomy that can be surmounted only by divine grace. That is why God sent his Son when the fullness of time came (Gal. 4, 6). Since then, God's

7

presence with us and our communion with him are incorporated within the sacramental structures of the Church.

But what about God's presence and man's communion with him in the days of preparation? What was the situation in Old Testament times and before? These are the questions that will concern us in this article.

I

PRE-BIBLICAL RELIGIONS

The message of the Old Testament was, in large part, a response to the paganism surrounding it. But does this mean that pre-biblical religions were totally without value? To answer this question we must consider the objective data provided by the history of religions.

1. *Data from the History of Religions*

The man of antiquity (who survives today in certain traditional civilizations) had an acute awareness of the sacred. He saw the sacred present in all the realities of the cosmos and in all aspects of his social life; he thus interpreted them as hierophancies.[1] Within the framework of this total sacralization, his representation of the "divine" logically took as many shapes as human experience could suggest. There is no need to stress this point; it lies at the root of the many and varied mythologies.

Finding himself in the presence of supernatural realities at every turn, man sought to make peace with them, to secure the benefits that each deity had to offer, and even to go so far as to be absorbed within them.[2] This was the essential aim of cultic worship, which was much more than simple adoration of the deity. Cultic rites, endowed with quasi-magical efficacy, made

---

[1] The expression is that of M. Eliade, *Traité d'histoire des religions* (Paris, 1949).

[2] This is the orientation of Plotinian and Hindu mysticism, both being relatively independent of the cults in which they arose.

real man's relationship to the powers above by depicting it in symbolic form. In this framework we can understand the pertinence of sacred places, sacrifices, ritual meals, etc.

Thus the sacral quality of the ancient world was somewhat peculiar. The divine shone forth everywhere, and everywhere man found an opportunity to establish a relationship with it. But this sacral quality was vague and ambiguous, because the notion of God could hardly be disentangled from the cosmic and social environment in which man found himself enmeshed.

It is easy to see why biblical revelation could not endorse this particular view of the sacred. The fundamental notion would have to be clarified first.

2. Revelation Confronts the Pagan Religions

To affirm its originality over against paganism, the religion of the Old Testament vigorously denounced the prevailing ambiguity surrounding the sacred. To be sure, it did admit that in the world and outside it there were benevolent and malevolent powers who could intervene here below. But it maintained that the name "God" had to be reserved for the unique being who revealed himself to the patriarchs and continued to speak through his prophets. No other power in heaven or on earth rated any cultic worship: that was the first commandment of the Decalogue (Ex. 20, 2-3).

The result was to root out and eliminate the myths, which scattered divinity among a host of agents, and the concomitant rites, which put man in communication with the gods. From this standpoint, revelation's judgment on paganism was totally negative. What is more, by stressing the transcendence of the one God, revelation seemed to increase the distance between him and man. With its acute awareness of sin, revelation made it more difficult for man to have access to God. While still allowing for the possibility of contemplating God and communicating with him through the prophetic function, it cut short every attempt to experience the divine directly. There would be no more orgiastic mysticism in which man felt himself imbued with the obscure powers of the cosmos. There could be no return to the source of being, no immersion in the pristine cosmic principle.

God was not to be confused with some notion of mother nature in whose bosom man developed. There could be no favorable judgment on the worship of "strange gods". Membership in the People of God required that there first be *a complete break* from the customs of other peoples.

But here and there in the Old Testament we find a different vein of thought. Genesis 4—11 indicates that even before the call of Abraham God found sincere worshippers in the pagan world: Abel, Henoch, Noah, and others. They are legendary figures, to be sure, but their importance does not depend on their historical authenticity. They are important for what they represent in the history of God's relationship with man: even in paganism a handful of just men found a way to worship the true God in a fitting manner.

Henoch and Noah "walked with God" (Gen. 5, 22; 6, 9): the phrase connotes an atmosphere of familiarity, where man knows he is accompanied by God's presence. Abel and Noah offered sacrifices that were pleasing to God (Gen. 4, 4; 8, 21); in short, the symbolic rites of the traditional cults could have a correct sense and real efficacy, if they were performed by upright men. Moreover, the story of Noah indicates that even in prehistoric times man lived in a covenant economy, with the signs of God's benevolence inscribed in the cosmos (Gen. 9, 12-16).

But Abel, Henoch and Noah (like the three just men cited in Ezekiel 14, 14) were exceptions. The rest of humanity around them remained far from God, having lost all precise knowledge of him (cf. Rom. 1, 21). Their cults were enmeshed in lies: they sacrificed to demons who were not God at all (Dt. 37, 17), and they ate at their table (1 Cor. 10, 20).

II
SIGNS OF GOD IN THE OLD COVENANT

The faith of Israel looked for signs of God's presence in a domain that pagan mythologies had not sacralized: the domain of history.[3]

1. God's Presence in History

The word of God came to man through the intermediary of the prophetic message. (Here we use the word "prophetic" in the broadest sense.) In so doing, it became a *happening* inscribed in a particular time context and a particular set of circumstances. Moreover, its content was not concerned solely with the essence of God in its non-temporal purity; it was also concerned with the action of God in time and the carrying out of his salvation plan within history.

God revealed himself through his actions, directing the course of events which make up the fabric of human experience. To be sure, the interpretation of events would be impossible without the prophetic word that lies behind it; but the prophetic utterance would lack substance if it were not meant to highlight God's involvement in the realm of history.[4]

Finally, the prophetic word must be *accredited by signs* if it is to enkindle faith in men's hearts. The sign could be a miracle, in the modern sense of that word. But it could also be a faith-inspired realization of the meaning imbedded in events themselves, without the "laws of nature" being involved at all. In the Old Testament it is often difficult to trace the boundary between the two types of signs. Both manifested the presence of God in history.

Here we might mention a whole series of events that Israel

[3] M. Eliade, *Le mythe de l'éternel retour* (Paris, 1949), pp. 152ff: "L'Histoire considérée come théophanie."

[4] Constitution *Dei Verbum*, n. 2: "The economy of revelation comprises deeds and words that are intimately tied up with one another."

preserved in memory and pondered in order to decipher the ways of God. They started with the vocation of Abraham and reached their climax in the golden age of the nation under David and Solomon. In this human drama, quite similar to that of many other nations, faith discerned a connecting thread that tied all the incidents together. God had summoned the fathers of the Israelite nation and given them his promises. He fulfilled these promises by making Israel his own people, by giving them the covenant, the law and the holy land, by delivering them from their enemies and allowing them to grow into a powerful monarchy. These divine actions were tangible proof of God's favor toward his people (cf. Pss. 78, 105, 106).

The exodus from Egypt was the sign par excellence, in which Israel recognized the "powerful hand" of her God. Through it "the people stood in awe of the Lord and trusted the Lord and his servant Moses" (Ex. 14, 31). God was ever present in the wings of history, directing its course. Without losing their empirical reality, all historical events provided practical experience in the ways of God.

In using this key to interpret Israel's sojourn in the desert, biblical tradition paid special attention to those details where God's presence was most tangible. (We shall return to the Sinai covenant later, noting its cultic format.) The simple fact that they had found sufficient food and water in the desert became a concrete sign of God's attentiveness for all succeeding generations (Ex. 17, 1-7; 16, 2-36; picked up again in Pss. 78, 15-24; 105, 40-41).

To be sure, various texts embellished the details of the original experience, which are presented quite prosaically in other texts. Numbers 11, 7-8 describes the manna quite prosaically, while the book of Wisdom talks about "angels' food . . . strong in all enjoyment and suited to every taste" (Wis. 16, 20). But this literary development serves to enhance the import of the experience, and St. Paul sees anticipated in it the presence of God's Spirit: "All ate the same supernatural food and all drank the same supernatural drink" (1 Cor. 10, 3). Need we point out that

Deuteronomy interprets the rich fruits of the promised land in a similar perspective (Dt. 8, 7-10; 26, 9-10)?

Encounter with God, then, does not represent an escape from the material world at all. Instead it embraces even the most material aspects of human existence.

2. Communion with God in Cultic Worship

The cultic worship of the Old Testament reveals its originality, not in the rites it performs, but in the faith which inspires it. Through its affirmation of monotheism, the sacred lost its ambiguity and no longer resulted in the quasi-divinization of creatures.

Yahweh is the one and only God (Dt. 6, 4), and he alone merits cultic worship (Dt. 6, 13). But since God has taken the initiative to approach man and establish a relationship with him, man must respond to the summons of God's word with acts of his own. The account of the covenant sealed on Sinai dominates both the law and cultic worship. The ratification of the covenant (Ex. 24, 3-8) is presented as a twofold ritual, which corresponds to the two sources utilized in the extant narrative.

On the one hand, the obligation of the people to observe the terms of the covenant is solemnly ratified by the holocaust, the sacrifices, and the sprinkling of blood (Ex. 24, 3-8). On the other hand, the leaders of the community, led by Moses, are brought into God's presence and commune with him in a sacred meal (Ex. 24, 1-2. 9-11). Thus *the meaning of the covenant* is explicitated from two points of view: it is man's response to the word which God has already addressed to him; and it is also man's entry into familiarity with God, who now communicates his life to his people. When we examine the cultic institutions of the Old Testament, we must never lose sight of these two aspects of cultic worship.

Celebration of a cultic ritual would be devoid of value if it did not spring from a living faith that is nourished by the word of God. This explains the anti-cultic diatribes that we find in the prophets (Am. 5, 21-27; Is. 1, 10-16; Jer. 6, 20) and in the liturgical prayers of the psalter (Pss. 50; 51, 18-19). The rites have value only when they express an interior attitude of faith and obedience to God's word. If this attitude is present, then the rites accomplish what they purport to do. Every aspect of man's corporeal and social life is caught up in the religious relationship, of which faith is the heart.

Within this basic context, Israel picked up the traditional gestures that expressed man's reverence for the godhead and his desire to enter into communion with it. But now it was no longer a question of cosmic deities; cultic worship was directed to the transcendent God who "spoke and it was made" (Ps. 33, 9). He continued to dwell in the sanctuary, which remained as a souvenir of the Sinai covenant and eventually eclipsed all the other sanctuaries (2 Kgs. 23, 1-20). From the tent in the desert to the temple of Jerusalem, it was the permanent sign of God's presence, the place where God's glory dwells. In approaching this sanctuary, man could truly say that he had come to "behold the face of God"; the expression crops up in many psalms (cf. Pss. 42, 2; 63, 3).

In general, all the sacred rites expressed the same fundamental religious notion, and this notion was couched in covenant terms. Various rites expressed various aspects of the same notion. On the one hand, man directed his homage to God through holocausts, sacrifices and acts of thanksgiving; these things accomplished what they expressed in symbolic form. In return, God received his faithful people at his own table (cf. Ps. 23, 5) in a communion sacrifice which followed the sacred meal; they became cognizant of his nearness to them. When this sacrifice was part of a feast commemorating some event in salvation history, the participants felt somehow associated with the original event that they were commemorating. Passover was a notable instance of this.

Thus, cultic worship occupied an essential place in man's search for communion with God. Man had to arrive at this goal by using symbols from the world of sense experience and imagination to make contact with a God who lay far beyond this realm.

3. *The Religious Meaning of the Universe*

Rooted in prophetic utterances and historical experiences, revelation then turned back to the domain which had captivated the ancient mythologies: the domain of the cosmos.[5] The God of history was also the creator of the world; in him the universe found its existence, its harmony and its meaning. No longer divinized, temporal realities could now serve as signs of God's presence (cf. Pss. 19; 104). The grandiose spectacle of nature and cosmic forces is no longer an ambiguous hierophany but a triumphant theophany (cf. Pss. 18, 8-18; 29; 77, 17-19, etc.). The language of myth was now shot through with faith, and it was used to express a different outlook.

Revelation was strong enough to adopt this mode of expression in order to bring out the true sacral nature of things. But it now plays a subordinate role, because everything is transformed and recast here, too. For God's presence in the cosmos and in history *becomes real for each individual in the word* which is addressed to him as a summons to faith. It is here that the nearness of God is verified: "For what great nation is there that has a god so near to it as the Lord our God is to us, whenever we call upon him?" (Dt. 4, 7). "But the word is very near to you; it is in your mouth and in your heart, so that you can do it" (Dt. 30, 14).

III

THE PROBLEM OF HUMAN SIN

Here we run up against the critical problem of human sin, which stands as an obstacle to man's communion with God. We need not retrace the development of this concept (sin) in the Old Testament.[6] The Law, an essential element in the covenant economy, played a major role in the process.

[5] E. Beaucamp, *La Bible et le sens religieux de l'univers,* Lectio Divina 25 (Paris, 1959).

[6] Cf. "Théologie biblique du péché," in *Supplément de la Vie Spirituelle* (1962), pp. 204-221.

Confronted by the word which spelled out God's will, Israel
wished to remain mindful of her sinful state. In this she was not
always successful. Aside from idolatry, there was always a temptation to give way to empty ritualism. The intervention of the
prophets was to play a decisive role here.

Isaiah 1, 1-16 describes God's reaction to a cultic ritual that no
longer had any real meaning. He was shocked and nauseated by
it. The people's hands were full of blood, and their offerings were
vain; they would have to wash themselves clean and cease to do
evil (Is. 1, 15-16).

1. *The Limits of the Old Economy*

But was such a conversion possible? Could the people have a
change of heart? Some of the prophets seemed to think so, but
Jeremiah shattered this illusion (cf. Jer. 7, 27-28): "Can the
Ethiopian change his skin or the leopard his spots? Then also
you can do good who are accustomed to do evil" (Jer. 13, 23).
Israel's sinfulness reveals her incapacity to live up to the covenant; the covenant will break up, like a marriage broken up
because of adultery (cf. Hos. 2). *The spiritual drama of the
chosen people is a concrete expression of the condition of the
whole human race.* Even God's gifts seem powerless in the face
of man's hardheartedness.

In this state of affairs the sinful community will be deprived of
the terrestrial riches which it had been promised conditionally.
But that is not all. It will also experience the *absence of God;* in
other words, God will become its judge and almost its enemy.
The prophetic passages announcing divine judgment and catas-
trophic tragedy are disconcerting to anyone who is looking for
descriptions of mystical experience in the Old Testament.

What, then, is man in God's eyes? In his inaugural vision,
Isaiah himself is struck with terror at his own impurity (Is. 6, 5).
Sinful humanity should not be surprised to find a barrier between
God and itself, and Israel is part of that humanity. Suddenly the
old covenant finds itself checkmated, and we have reached an
important dialectical moment in the revelation of God's salvific

plan. Notice that it is not a defeat for God, because he is also the judge who passes sentence on Israel. In decreeing a tragic destiny for her, he reveals his presence in history in a different manner. But there is something in man that is an obstacle to God's plan; he will have to get around this obstacle in order to carry out his designs.

2. *The Eschatological Promises*

Over against their prophecies of divine chastisement, the prophets proclaim divine promises of salvation at the very end of history. Such themes as the coming of God, God's presence among men and man's communion with him, take on considerable importance. To give them an aura of concreteness, the prophets incorporate the major traits of past history which express the same ideas. This literary technique injects into eschatology the symbols that had been part and parcel of Israel's history and Israel's institutions.

To begin with, the events that had made up the fulfillment of God's plan (from the exodus to the possession of the promised land, and from the Sinai covenant to the golden age of the monarchy) are now projected into the future. The first plan of God had not attained fulfillment; the new plan would incorporate the fundamental structures of the first plan, eliminating the obstacles that had brought the first to nought.

In the book of Hosea, the promise of a new covenant is developed as an allegory on marriage (Hos. 2). The heart of the prophecy is the enumeration of the spiritual gifts that God will give his spouse (i.e., his people): righteousness and justice, steadfast love and mercy, fidelity and knowledge of God (2, 20). But this does not eliminate the existence of concrete signs that depict the return to grace on an experiential level. The book of Jeremiah, too, describes the new covenant in very refined terms (Jer. 31, 31-34); but the return to the promised land still maintains a place in his panorama of salvation (Jer. 31, 10-14).

In the book of consolation (Is. 40-55), where the covenant theme is depicted as a marriage allegory (Is. 54), the time-honored experiences of the Sinai desert are projected into his portrait of the future. God will nourish his people, giving them food and drink (Is. 41, 17-20; 48, 20-21; 49, 9b-10).

Clearly we must take care to understand this kind of language aright. Only the eventual realization of God's plan in the future will show us exactly how these promises fit into the final picture. But they should participate in such a way that their realistic and physical dimensions are not reduced to pure abstractions; the sense dimension of man should have some place in the final picture.

In developing a theme borrowed from Ezekiel (Ez. 43, 1-7), the book of consolation provides a very concrete description of the eschatological revelation of God's glory (Is. 40, 5; 52, 8). Following the same vein of thought, Isaiah 60 describes a luminous theophany in which the new Jerusalem receives its brightness directly from God himself (Is. 60, 1-3. 19-20). Here cosmic symbolism is put in the service of another theme, "the God who is coming", in accordance with the techniques of liturgical poetry (cf. Pss. 18, 8-15; 50, 3; 97, 2-4). Thus demythologized creation provides its own complement of symbols to talk about the ineffable God.

But the essential point is on another level entirely. It concerns the religious tie between God and man. Man is not content to contemplate God; he is placed in a relationship of intimacy with him. The place accorded to cultic worship in the prophetic promises brings this out clearly.

In the book of Ezekiel, the ratification of the new covenant ties two events together: the gift of a new heart of flesh (Ez. 36, 26-27) is associated with a ritual aspersion of clean water (Ez. 36, 25). This same prophet goes into minute detail about the institutions required for the new cultic worship (Ez. 40—48). We should not be surprised, therefore, to see the Apocalypse of Isaiah (Is. 24—27) establish a close connection between the final revelation of God's glory and the temple (24, 23). It then goes on to describe eschatological joy in terms of a cultic festival, to which God invites all the nations of the earth (25, 6). The definitive transformation of the human condition (Is. 25, 7-8; cf. 65, 19) will result from this new-found access to communion with God.

IV
BIBLICAL TYPOLOGY AND NEW TESTAMENT REALITY

Our previous comments indicate how the Christian notion of biblical types gradually took shape in the Old Testament.[7] It was not a process of abstract speculation, using artificial symbolism and arbitrarily attaching it to objects that did not originally have any such import.

1. *The Roots of Typology*

This typology was rooted in the existential experience of Israel, wherein she glimpsed the plan of God in action. Thus, it is clear to see why a privileged place was accorded to those past events that formed part of the salvation experience. While he is discussing the events of the exodus, Paul enunciates his basic principle: "Now all these things happened to them as a type" (1 Cor. 10, 11).

Cosmic symbolism now takes a subordinate place. It is no longer simply a matter of pointing out that God stands in the background of reality; it is now a matter of pointing out that God comes to man in the context of history to establish a relationship with him.[8] Cultic rites can be interpreted in one of two ways, depending on whether they are part of a cosmic religion or an historical religion. The Old Testament borrowed its rites from cosmic religion and reinterpreted them in the framework of an historical religion; it integrated the former into the latter. That is why its cultic actions, symbolizing an encounter with a

---

[7] See my treatment in *Sens chrétien de l'Ancien Testament,* pp. 209-47, 286-326; *La Bible, Parole de Dieu,* pp. 265-287.

[8] But there is a typology of creation (insofar as it is an act of God) and of the original paradise (insofar as it evokes the intention of the creator): cf. *Sens chrétien de l'Ancien Testament,* pp. 384-88.

God "who is coming", also serve as types for the great eschatological encounter.

By transferring Israel's historical and liturgical symbolism into
the domain of eschatology, the prophets initiated the development of biblical typology. Their oracles are couched in a language that can be called figurative.[9] It reveals and conceals at
the same time, using the past to unveil the future but presuppos-
ing that all the earlier limits will be surpassed and overcome.

The New Testament will pick up this language to express the
original and astounding content of the Christian experience. This
content is rooted in the incarnation of the Son of God, and the
New Testament explicitates it as if it flowed naturally from the
symbolic structures that had been prepared in the Old Testament
—despite its utter novelty.

Thus, Israel's history and cultic worship occupy a place in
her life of faith that is homologous to the place of Christ and his
mysteries in Christian faith. This similarity is the criterion of
authentic typology.[10]

2. *Anticipations of the Christian Experience*

However, it is faith that gives continuity to this whole experience, that allows us to pass from type to the reality prefigured by
it. It all begins when God first speaks to man, and it reaches
fulfillment in Christ, the Word made flesh. From the Old Testament on, it is faith which allows man to respond to God's word,
to interpret history correctly, and to give authentic meaning to
his cultic worship.

In the Word of God, the manifestation of his wisdom, *man
already experiences an encounter with the living God*. It is an
obscure experience, to be sure, lacking the visible character of
historical events and the sense dimension of cultic ritual. Yet
God is present there, accosting man and directing his summons
to him; and to the extent that man accepts this word, God enters
into direct communication with him.

[9] *Ibid.*, pp. 363-403.
[10] *La Bible, Parole de Dieu*, pp. 284-86.

Thus God's word is food and drink for man (Is. 55, 1-3). Wisdom prepares a sacred banquet for man, which is mirrored weakly and only symbolically in his own cultic meals (Prov. 9, 1-6). Man makes direct contact with a transcendent presence which, in itself, lies beyond the realm of images. The Word has not yet revealed himself in the world, but already he is communicating something of himself in this divine word. His entrance into the world is already foreshadowed in the word of God.[11] This is the mysterious reality which accounts for the meaning that faith sees in historical and cultic experience.

The psalmist sometimes talks about the presence of God in terms of cultic worship. But it should not surprise us that he usually describes it in terms of his own interior life, where the word of God plays a central role. He loves the law of God and delights in it (Pss. 119; 70; 97; 103; etc). His only desire is to dwell in the house of the Lord and to behold his beauty (Pss. 27, 4; 34, 9). He longs for God alone (Ps. 73, 25-26), who can guarantee the fullness of joy to man (Ps. 16, 11). This is *lived faith,* which gives authentic meaning to historical events and cultic actions. Thanks to it, God can be said to be *present under the veil of types.*

Consider the story of the manna and the cultic meal. They do not foreshadow the future Christian experience simply because they deal with food and nourishment. Aside from the nourishment, some sort of divine presence is perceived by faith. And is it not faith that allows us to receive Christ today as the bread of life, rejoicing even more than our forefathers who ate manna in the desert (Jn. 6, 47-50)?

Here we have the real eschatological banquet that was foretold by the prophets and awaited by the Hebrews; but how different the reality is from any human expectations! Here we have the banquet of which wisdom speaks, and the invitation is open to all who are ready to believe (Apoc. 3, 20). But this banquet, too, is translated into sacramental terms, for faith must invest the whole man—including his senses and his imagination. That is why

[11] *Sens chrétien de l'Ancien Testament,* pp. 132-34.

Christ has turned his flesh and blood into our food and drink (Jn. 6, 53-55).

This new ritual meal is a prolongation of the last supper and a memorial of the cross. But those who take part in it do not experience the same fate as the Hebrews in the desert: "Your forefathers ate the manna and died; whoever eats this bread will live forever" (Jn. 6, 59).

Thomas Barrosse, C.S.C./*Rome, Italy*

The Passover and the Paschal Meal

For the ancient Semitic world a meal, especially a communal meal, had a significance which modern man often fails to appreciate. Table fellowship, for example, implied commitment to tablemates, and this rendered eating and drinking together an apt way of sealing a covenant (Gen. 31, 54; Ex. 24, 3; Tob. 7, 11-15) and made betrayal by a tablemate a particularly perfidious act (Ps. 41 [40], 10).

The sacred was already present in the important, mysterious and symbolism-filled act of taking nourishment. It would be all the more present in a meal taken in a sacred context. Already as early as the period of the Judges, one of the most popular acts of Israelite cult was the "communion sacrifice" or "peace offering", in which part of an animal was burned on an altar and part was cooked and eaten by the offerer. The worshippers certainly felt that this meal brought them into communion not only with one another in a particularly solemn fashion but also and especially with the divinity.

Exactly how they thought this communion with their God was effected, however, is not clear. Did they feel they were sharing a meal with him? Some of their neighbors understood sacrificial cult as a feeding of the gods. But in Israel, at least in a later period, what was laid on the altar was not even considered an

23

edible portion (Lev. 3, 3f.; 7, 22-27), and Old Testament authors insisted repeatedly that Israel's God had no need of what his worshippers brought. Did they feel they were in communion with God because they consumed something sacred (cf. Lev. 7, 11-21)? Their neighbors certainly felt that this was a way of effecting communion with the divinity. But the Old Testament writings never refer to the meat eaten by the participants in a sacred meal as "holy", although this adjective does describe the edible portions reserved to the priests in various sacrifices. In any case, the immolated animal was, in a sense, shared with the divinity since part of it was burned and, what is perhaps more important, the meal was taken in a sacred context. Whatever the precise reason, Israelites recognized this rite as a privileged means of communion with the covenant God.

The sacred meal most deserving of attention in the Old Testament is the paschal supper. It would, however, be a mistake to regard it simply as a particular kind of "communion sacrifice". Although it was early assimilated to this rite (Ex. 12, 27; 23, 18; 34, 25), the two may very well have had quite independent origins.

I

PRE-MOSAIC ORIGINS

Mosaic religion assimilated a sizable number of pagan cult practices. The feasts of the spring barley harvest (Unleavened Bread), the wheat harvest (Weeks or Pentecost), and the end of the farming year in the fall (Booths or Ingathering) are examples of Canaanite agricultural observances adopted by the Yahwist cult: they became the occasion of celebrations at the sanctuaries of the covenant God and were eventually considered to be commemorative of his great saving acts—respectively, of the deliverance from Egypt (perhaps already in the time of the Judges), the giving of the Law at Sinai (about the close of the Old Testament period), and the providential guidance during the desert wanderings (at least by the time of the Babylonian exile).[1]

The passover, too, was doubtless a pre-Mosaic rite. Exodus 5, 1-3 and 10, 8f. may be evidence that the people were already familiar with a passover-like practice well before the moment for their departure from Egypt. In any case, the origins of the passover seem certainly to antedate the establishment of Yahwism in Canaan. The rite as described in Exodus 12 supposes a nomadic rather than a sedentary way of life. The use of sheep and goats to the exclusion of larger animals, the preparatory isolation of the animal from the flock presumably as its first fruits in the spring, the manner of preparing and eating it with quickly baked unleavened bread and easily gathered herbs, the nocturnal celebration by families attired as nomads ready for the march rather than in larger groups—all point to an origin among a people not yet settled down to an agricultural way of life. Besides, this single detailed Old Testament description of the paschal ritual exhibits striking parallels with practices that have survived to the present century among nomadic Arab groups, especially the use of the blood of the animal eaten. Finally, the people are told to observe a passover *for Yahweh*—a phrase suggesting that the innovation of Exodus 12 lies rather in the purpose of the observance than in any novelty of ritual.[2]

Any attempt to conjecture what the pre-Mosaic rite was like and what it meant must be based on Exodus 12 in view of the all but total absence of other Old Testament descriptions. Though the passage belongs to the most recent of the four great Pentateuchal sources, we can safely base our speculations upon it: the

[1] For Unleavened Bread see the Yahwist and Elohist calendars (Ex. 34, 28; 23, 15), for Booths see the Priestly calendar (Lev. 23, 42f.), and for Weeks see G. Moore, *Judaism in the First Centuries of the Christian Era* II (Cambridge, 1935), p. 48 and R. De Vaux, *Ancient Israel. Its Life and Institutions* (London, 1961), p. 494.

[2] See H. Haag, "Pâque," in *Dict. Bible. Suppl.* VI for the passover-like rites outside Israel. He summarizes remarks of É. Dhorme, *La religion des Hébreux nomades* (Bruxelles, 1937); J. Henninger, "Les fêtes du printemps chez les Arabes et leurs implications historiques," in *Revista do Museu paulista* 4 (1950) pp. 389-432; and A. Jaussen, *Coutumes des Arabes au pays de Moab* (Paris, 1948).

Priestly source faithfully preserves very ancient usages, and the nomadic character of the rite it presents warrants our supposition that it is doing so here.

The name "passover" (*pesah*) unfortunately sheds little light on the meaning of the observance. The noun occurs exclusively as the name of the rite or the animal used in it. The cognate adjective and verb signify limping and, except for three instances, do not refer to the passover observance. In Exodus 12 the verb occurs three times (vv. 13, 23, 27) of Yahweh, who, in passing through the land to strike the Egyptians down, "passes over" (?) the houses or doors of the Israelites' dwellings to avoid striking them or to protect them from destruction. In Isaiah 31, 5 the verb also occurs of Yahweh, but without any clear reference to the passover observance: he will "pass over" (or "spare"?) and deliver Jerusalem.

Exodus 12 describes a nocturnal rite comprising the smearing of blood on the entrance to a family dwelling and a communal eating of the meat of the animal from which the blood came by all the dwelling's inhabitants. Blood, the fluid in which life was felt to reside (Gen. 9, 4; Lev. 17, 11), has a mysterious and even sacred character in the Old Testament. It could not be eaten but had to be poured against the altar or onto the ground (Lev. 7, 26f.; 17, 3f., 10-14) and was used to purify and sanctify (Lev. 8; 16; cf. Ex. 24, 5-8). The smearing of blood on the entrance to the dwelling in the pre-Mosaic passover was doubtless meant to ward off evil influences. Night, we would surmise, was the time when they were most active just as, for the Old Testament, the desert was the place where they dwelt (Lev. 16, 8-10, 21f.; Tob. 8, 1-3; cf. Is. 34, 14 for the night demon Lilith). If we ask on what occasion the ritual might have been used, the answer suggested by Exodus 12 is the start of a journey, perhaps any camp-breaking, perhaps some sort of pilgrimage, perhaps a spring migration. In any case, a likely conclusion is that the blood rite and the communal meal were used to bind the family together and protect it against the disruptive forces that might threaten it as it uprooted itself and set out on its way.

II
THE PASSOVER AND THE EXODUS

According to Exodus 12, this rite was intimately involved in the deliverance of Israel from Egyptian captivity preparatory to the covenant-making at Sinai—the series of events which created Israel or brought them into existence as Yahweh's special possession (Ex. 6, 6f.; 19, 4-6). Hence, the month in which it occurred was to be kept as the beginning of their year (Ex. 12, 2). The blood saved the families whose dwellings were marked with it on the night on which Yahweh passed through the land to strike every household with death. The meal presumably bound the members of the family together as they prepared their departure from the place of bondage and exposed themselves to the dangers and disruptive forces of an unpredictable journey into the desert. In short, the rite served to set Israel apart—apart from the Egyptians and apart as the community which Yahweh redeemed and made his own.

The same chapter of Exodus prescribes the observance of the anniversary of this night through the repetition of the rite by the entire community of Israel in all their generations forever. A permanent institution of Mosaic religion, it was to serve as a "memorial" of Israel's departure from Egypt. This term, of course, does not mean a mere reminder of the past. The verb "to remember" occurs regularly in the Old Testament in a pregnant sense: to take cognizance of a situation with a view to reacting to it. God, for example, "remembers" his covenant with the patriarchs in order to fulfill it (Ex. 2, 24; 6, 5). He is asked to remember his promise of pardon and help for his repentant people in order to keep it (Neh. 1, 8f.). His not remembering sins means his pardoning them (Is. 43, 25). Man remembers the sabbath to keep it holy (Ex. 20, 8) or God's deeds to praise them (Ps. 77 [76], 12).

In Exodus, 12, 14 the passover "memorial" seems to be the

community's remembrance of the past events rather than the community's reminding Yahweh of them. In favor of the latter position, it could be noted that Old Testament prayers often remind the covenant God of his past benefits with a view to obtaining a further manifestation of his benevolence and that in Exodus 12, 13 the blood on the doorposts is a sign to indicate to Yahweh that the house so marked is to be spared. But precisely this part of the original passover ritual did not survive in the yearly repetition, and in Exodus 13 the people are told that *they* must remember the day of their deliverance to keep the observances prescribed for it (v. 3) and that practices related to it are a "memorial" meant to keep Yahweh's law in *their* minds (v. 9). Finally, the passover ritual itself is supposed to provide the occasion for an explanation of Yahweh's redemption of his people to their children (Ex. 12, 26f.).

A ritual *meal*, however, can hardly be a reminder in the same way in which practices like abstinence from leavened bread (Ex. 13, 9), dedication of the firstborn to Yahweh (Ex. 13, 16), the wearing of fringes on a garment (Num. 15, 39), or the public reading of the Law (Deut. 31, 10-13) were to keep the people mindful of their responsibility to their God. Perhaps the way to an understanding of the passover as a memorial lies along the lines indicated by Deuteronomy: the Israelites of each generation had to regard themselves not simply as members of a people which Yahweh had called into existence in the past but as personally delivered by him and made partners to his covenant (Dt. 5, 2f.; 29, 13f.). The meal would, like any meal, be a means of renewing the bonds that kept the members of the community of Israel together. As a meal that was eaten in memory of the great saving deed of their God and in imitation of the one they had eaten at the moment of this intervention, it would be a means of renewing the bond that kept them together as his redeemed people. It would, in a sense, be a means of communicating with that past event or in its effects.

III
LATER DEVELOPMENTS

Over the centuries the passover observance maintained itself with extraordinary stability despite the developments it underwent and the interpretations it was given. The earliest development after the establishment in Canaan seems to have been its association with the spring agricultural celebration of Unleavened Bread, which had itself become a reminder of the exodus from Egypt. The oldest liturgical calendars do not associate the two observances (Yahwist calendar: Ex. 34, 18. 25; Elohist: Ex. 23, 15. 18), but the authors of Deuteronomy (16, 1-8. 16) and Ezekiel (45, 21-24) show themselves unaware of any distinction between them.

The confusion of Passover with Unleavened Bread, which was a pilgrimage feast, tended to make it a sanctuary celebration and jeopardized its survival as a ritual to be observed in every Israelite family. Deuteronomy 16, 1-8 made it just such a celebration (vv. 5-7), permitting the use of the larger animals immolated at the cult center (v. 2) and apparently extending it over more than a single night (v. 3 in contrast with v. 4). Its assimilation to the "communion sacrifice" (Ex. 12, 27; 23, 18; 34, 25; cf. Dt. 16, 2) posed the same threat, at least from the moment that Josiah's Deuteronomic reform limited sacrificial cult to the Jerusalem temple. The ritual meal could be eaten with the meat of a sacrificed animal only in Jerusalem, where it would be possible to immolate a victim at the temple and consume it on the same evening. Outside Jerusalem and, after the destruction of the temple, even within the city, the paschal supper would have to be taken without the animal. The family celebration, however, survived these threats and maintained itself, though without the paschal victim, presumably because it was a practice deeply rooted among the people and of great significance to them.

Various meanings were seen in the observance at different periods or by different writers. The Priestly source of the Pentateuch, to which we owe the bulk of Exodus 12, mentions two passovers, each at the start of a journey: in Egypt as Israel prepared to set out for the mountain where the covenant would be made (Ex. 12) and a year later at Sinai as the newly organized community prepared to break camp and start its trek across the desert toward the promised land (Num. 9, 1-14).

The Deuteronomist history also mentions two passovers, which serve as the high points at the start and the finish of the story it recounts and are both meant to be new beginnings. After crossing the Jordan into the land of promise as their parents had crossed the Sea of Reeds, the generation of Israelites born in the desert was circumcised by Joshua and celebrated the passover; thereupon the manna ceased, and they began to live off the produce of Canaan (Jos. 4, 19—5, 12). After implementing his great Deuteronomic reform, suppressing all illegitimate cult, and renewing the covenant with Yahweh, Josiah held a passover in Jerusalem, the like of which had never been seen since the days of the Judges, that is, since the time of Joshua (2 Kgs. 23, 22). This was the triumph of Deuteronomic religion but it came too late to save the people from exile.

The chronicler sees a passover celebrated by men from Israel and Judah as closely tied in with the three great renewals of the temple cult by the line of David. He presents a somewhat irregular passover celebration as the high point of Hezekiah's religious reform (2 Chron. 30),[3] a passover observance without parallel since the start of the monarchy as the climax of Josiah's reform (2 Chron. 35, see especially v. 18), and a passover celebrated at the dedication of the temple rebuilt under the Davidic prince Zerubbabel (Ezra 6) as the first great step in the postexilic restoration, which was then completed by the refortification

[3] The month-late celebration (cf. Num. 9, 6-13) might have been planned to coincide with a traditional northern dating for the feast in order to attract people from the north: see 1 Kings 12, 32 for a northern celebration of Booths one month later than the Jerusalem practice.

of Jerusalem and the proclamation of the Law by Nehemiah and Ezra. The passover is connected with reform and renewal; the feast of Booths is reserved as the occasion for the original consecration of the temple (as in 1 Kgs. 8, 2) and for the proclamation of the Law to the postexilic community (compare 2 Chron. 7, 8-10 and Neh. 8, 17—9, 1). The passover seems to be for the chronicler the great renewal celebration when the community attempts to resume its efforts to realize this author's ideal of a united and observant Israel under Davidic rule centering its life about the Jerusalem temple.

The intertestamental and rabbinic literature witnesses to the central position which the passover observance held in the Jewish mind.[4] They identify the night of the passover meal as the anniversary of the creation of the world, the circumcision of Abraham, the sacrifice of Isaac, the entrance of Israel into Egypt, and the release of Joseph from prison. They consider it the night on which the saving events they still await will take place: the new exodus from captivity, the appearance of the Messiah, the coming of Moses and Elijah, the resurrection of the patriarchs and the end of the world. The association of so many past and future saving interventions of God with the passover night suggests that for Judaism it was *the* celebration of divine salvation. It also suggests how the observance could come to be looked upon not only as a "memorial" of their past for the people but as a reminder to their God of his promises. Since that night "was a night of watching on the part of Yahweh to bring them out of the land of Egypt, it is a night of watching for Yahweh on the part of all the children of Israel throughout their generations" (Ex. 12, 42).

[4] For the associations indicated in this paragraph see R. Le Déaut, *La nuit pascale* (Analecta Biblica, 22), (Rome, 1963), and N. Füglister, *Die Heilsbedeutung des Pascha* (Studien zum Alten und Neuen Testament, 8) (Munich, 1963). The Septuagint of Jeremiah 38, 8 (Heb. 31, 8) places the new exodus at the passover.

IV
THE JEWISH PASSOVER RITUAL

The description of the passover ritual found in the 2nd-century Mishnah, the early rabbinic legal tradition, purports to date in large part from before the destruction of the temple in 70 A.D. and, in all likelihood, does. It details the following procedure in its tractate on Passover (*Pesahim*).[5]

The slaughter of the animals began within the temple precincts well before twilight despite Exodus 12, 6 because of the great numbers. Each man slew the animal he had brought. (Thus, according to Philo,[6] each Israelite performed a priestly office on this day; however, slaying the victim was not the priest's office: see Leviticus 1—7.) The blood was dashed against the altar rather than used on the dwellings where the victims would be eaten, and parts of the animals were burned on the temple altar as in the "communion sacrifice" (cf. Lev. 3, 3f.). The passover victims were then roasted on spits of pomegranate wood.

The meal was to be eaten after nightfall, although the usual practice was to take the evening meal in late afternoon. It was to be eaten in a reclining position despite Exodus 12, 11 in accord with the Greco-Roman custom of the time and as befitted free men. It was eaten by families or small groups.

A first cup of wine was mixed, and God was blessed for both the feast and the cup. A preliminary dish was served and eaten before the usual table blessing and subsequent breaking of the bread with which Jewish meals ordinarily began. This was apparently intended, at least in part, to arouse the children's wonder.

Then the meal was set out, with its unusual menu of unleavened bread, bitter herbs, and, in Jerusalem, the paschal victim, and a second cup of wine was mixed. At this point, with every-

---

[5] For many details of rabbinic passover ritual which may help understanding of Jesus' paschal meal with the apostles in the gospels see J. Jeremias, *The Eucharistic Words of Jesus* (London, 1966).

[6] *Quaestiones in Exodum* 1, 10.

thing ready on the table, one of the children was expected to ask, "Why is this night different from all other nights?" and the father of the family provided the passover *haggadah,* that is, explanation or narrative, starting from Deuteronomy 26, 5-8: "My father was a wandering Aramean, and he went down into Egypt and sojourned there. . . . The Egyptians treated us harshly . . . and Yahweh brought us out of Egypt with a mighty hand and an outstretched arm. . . ."

Three things had to be explained: the passover victim, the unleavened bread and the bitter herbs as meaning respectively that God had passed over our fathers' houses in Egypt, our fathers were redeemed from Egypt and the Egyptians had made our fathers' lives bitter. But this evoking of the past was no mere recollection of events of long ago. In every generation each one had to regard himself as having personally come out of Egypt. So the narrative concluded with the recitation of the first part of the *Hallel,* those psalms of praise which sing of the Lord's greatness, his deliverance of the lowly, the exodus from Egypt and the triumph of those he sets free (Pss. 113—118 or, by the Greek and Latin numbering, 112—117). By the start of the 2nd century and possibly earlier, these prayers concluded with thoughts of future salvation. The second cup was drunk.

The bread was then broken, pieces distributed and the meal eaten in the usual way. Then a third cup of wine was mixed. Over this "cup of blessing" the grace after meals was recited, and it seems to have been passed around for all to drink from. Finally, over a fourth cup the remaining psalms of the *Hallel* were said.

This ritual is substantially the same as the one traced out in Exodus 12. Apart from minor accretions over the centuries, it remains the same today. A mere reading of it is enough to suggest the importance of the passover observance in the life of the people of Yahweh's covenant. During the earlier, agricultural period of Israel's history, the fall feast of Booths or Ingathering was the most popular, and it grew popular again after the exile; but its importance ultimately waned with social changes. At the sanctuaries the pilgrimage feasts enjoyed a certain preeminence, but this preeminence disappeared with the destruction of the temple. Passover was a family celebration and hence a less spectacular observance. But it was to be kept annually by the entire community of Israel and exclusively by them through all their generations. It was the rite by which they recalled the divine intervention that had set them free and made them Yahweh's own, the sacred meal by which they renewed and tightened the bonds that held them together as the people he had redeemed. Hence, it could be seen as the "memorial" of a host of other great past salvation events too (rabbinic literature), the occasion for a fresh start as covenant partners with the Lord (the Deuteronomist history and the chronicler), and the moment when the final great saving deed of God would be accomplished (intertestamental and rabbinic literature). In short, it was the privileged moment of communion between Israel and Israel's redeemer and between all the members of the people Yahweh had made his own.

Edward Kilmartin, S.J./*Weston, Massachusetts*

The Last Supper and the Earliest Eucharists of the Church

In the first century of the Christian era the expectation of the definitive establishment of the kingly rule of God was very much alive in Judaism. Jesus made it a key theme of his preaching but with this modification of the popular apocalyptic conception: The definitive kingly rule of God is not reserved for some new heavenly age but already breaks into history. This "good news" was concretized in the meals of Jesus' public life. In his preaching he speaks of the eschatological banquet native to the apocalyptic tradition and rooted in the Old Testament as something reserved for the future (Mt. 8, 11-12). On the other hand, the meals of Jesus' public life show a characteristic feature of the Messianic banquet which reveals in a dramatic way that through him God already begins to establish his kingdom among men.

It is typical of Jesus and his disciples not to fast but to hold joyous feasts. In answering the criticism leveled at this practice, Jesus says: "Can the wedding guests fast while the bridegroom is with them?" (Mk. 2, 19a). This is an authentic saying of Jesus and directly relates these meals to the banquet of the heavenly bridegroom mentioned in the parable of Mark 25, 1ff. Moreover, Jesus' custom of eating with publicans and sinners, a very unusual one, was clearly meant to signify the goal of the Messianic feast: union of sinful men with God. In answering the objection of the Pharisees to this practice, he simply says: "I have not come to call the righteous but sinners" (Mt. 9, 12; an authentic saying of Jesus).

I
LAST SUPPER

At the last supper Jesus makes explicit the meaning of his life and so the silent message of the meals of his public life: that he has come to destroy the barriers between sinful men and God. But he goes further and actually institutes the meal of the kingdom in its ecclesial dimension. In this connection the passover context is important. There are some doubts about whether the last supper coincided with the passover feast and the difficulty seems insoluble. At least it took place in the passover season. According to the synoptic accounts, Jesus intended this setting to serve as the occasion for the institution of a new cultic meal which would supplant the passover feast. This fact alone indicates that the synoptic writers understood this new meal to be the messianic meal in its ecclesial dimension. The feast of the passover, in the period approaching the Christian era, had become the most messianic of all Jewish feasts. There was a strong tradition that the Messiah would come and the kingdom and its banquet would be established at the passover. Being aware of this tradition, it is quite likely that the synoptic writers emphasized the passover setting so as to stress the eschatological character of this new meal.

Before considering the peculiar nature and form of this cultic meal, we may pause to observe the content of the *three eschatological sayings* linked to the words of institution (Lk. 22, 16. 18; Mk. 14, 25).

(a) There is some doubt about the authenticity of Luke 22, 16, but it may be an authentic saying of Jesus. Since v.15 could have the meaning of an unfulfilled desire regarding the eating of the meal, the saying of v.16 could have the meaning of a vow of abstinence. However, this interpretation is unacceptable for Mark 14, 18. 20 presupposes that Jesus ate the meal. This saying, therefore, must be interpreted simply as a declaration about the fulfillment of the kingdom in connection with an announcement of the death of Jesus (v.15).

(b) The second eschatological saying found in Luke 22, 18 is basically the same logion as Mark 14, 25.

(c) The position of the logion in Mark is more reliable. It is certainly an authentic saying of Jesus and in it the synoptic message about the kingdom finds its climactic expression: The end of the time of signs has come and the realization of the kingdom is imminent, where men will drink the messianic wine. However, events of momentous import must yet take place as a condition for the inauguration of the kingdom and its banquet. The nature of these events and their connection with the inauguration of the kingdom and its banquet are explained in the words of institution.

The four accounts of institution are liturgical adaptations of the *words* and *actions* of Jesus at the last supper.[1] The basic themes found in all the accounts are: vicarious expiation, covenant and the sharing of the messianic blessings through bread and wine. It is becoming increasingly evident that a satisfactory primordial text which would offer us the actual words used by Jesus at the last supper is beyond our reach. Nevertheless the basic themes ought to be attributed to Jesus since an analysis of the history of the formation of the liturgical accounts of institution gives no solid grounds for judging otherwise.

1. The Words

The theme of vicarious expiation is found in the bread saying of Paul/Luke and in the cup saying of Mark/Matthew. In all likelihood, the phrase "which is given for you" (Lk.) was found in the source of Mark's bread saying as interpretation of the meaning of body. The phrase in the cup saying, "which is shed for many" (Mk.), links Jesus with the Suffering Servant of Isaiah 53, 11-12. The term "many" refers to a totality and not a

[1] Mt. 26, 26-28; Mk. 14, 22-24; Lk. 22, 19-20; 1 Cor. 11, 24-25.

multitude in contrast to the whole. The Paul/Luke expression "for you" serves for immediate consolation and is due to liturgical influence; "for many" has the character of a confession.

In the post-biblical period the concept of non-ritual forms of expiation became popular among the Jews, chiefly under the form of suffering for personal sin. But also the possibility of vicarious suffering by the just man, as found in Isaiah 53, was widely accepted. Jesus explained the meaning of his death in terms of this type of expiation, with reference to Isaiah 53, and does not seem to have portrayed his death in an explicit way as antitype of the ritual sacrifices of the Old Law. In the bread saying of Paul/Luke, there is no reference to such a sacrificial concept. In Mark 14, 24 an allusion to ritual sacrifice arises from the combination of the themes of vicarious expiation and blood of the covenant (Ex. 24, 8). However, even granting the authenticity of Mark's cup saying, the sacrificial theme seems to be secondary. Here the basic idea is also that of vicarious expiation by the just man. To effect this the blood of Jesus is "shed for many": an expression which signifies a violent death in Jewish usage and is not immediately linked to the ritual sacrifice of Jewish cult.

In Jewish thought, expiation for sin is possible only because of God's positive ordinance. This is seen clearly in the case of expiatory sacrifices which are understood to have been established by God. The paradoxical thought, in line with this tradition, that it is God who grants vicarious expiation through Christ, abolishes his own judgment and saves men is well expressed in 2 Corinthians 5, 18: "God was in Christ reconciling the world to himself." In the words of institution Jesus expresses the same thought by using the passive voice: "my body which is given for you" (Lk.). If Jesus gives himself for mankind, it is because the Father has first given him to the world.

All the accounts of institution attribute to the death of Jesus the power to effect a covenant. In Mark the covenant is effected by the "shedding" of Jesus' blood; in Paul it is effected "in my blood" (i.e., in the power of my blood). The cup saying of Mark may be genuine for the objection that it cannot be rendered in Aramaic has been refuted. The Paul version can be explained on the basis of a desire to stress this covenant as fulfillment of the prophecy of Jeremiah 31, 31, which speaks of the "new covenant". However, the adjective "new" could not be introduced without a manipulation of the Aramaic text and a most readily available tranposition is precisely that found in 1 Corinthians 11, 25. There exists a rather common opinion that the association of the covenant theme with that of Suffering Servant was inspired by Isaiah 42, 6 and 49, 8, where the Servant is said to be given "as a covenant to the people". However, the only Old Testament texts alluded to are Exodus 24, 8 (possibly through Zechariah 9, 11) in Mark/Matthew and Jeremiah 31, 31 in Paul/Luke. The theme of covenant, therefore, seems to have arisen independently of the Servant theme and to have been linked with it by an original synthesis effected by Jesus himself.

The concept of a covenant with God is rooted in the Old Testament where it is based on the so-called suzerainty treaty: a relationship between unequal partners in which the stronger grants a covenant (*berîth*) to the weaker who, in turn, is obligated within definite boundaries. The covenant of Israel with Yahweh transcended all human covenants because it involved an order of salvation within which men formed their lives under the support and direction of Yahweh.

In using the concept of covenant Jesus reveals that by his death God will erect a new order of salvation in which men will share in the final *berîth* surpassing all others. The presentation of this concept together with that of expiation and the shedding of blood in Mark allows, as we have seen, for the death of Jesus to be viewed more as a cultic event reminiscent of Exodus 24, 8. In a later period it will be described as antitype of the Old Testament sacrifices, and legitimately so, in the Epistle to the Hebrews. The Paul cup saying expresses the idea that the covenant is established "in the power of Jesus' blood". This expression, however, does not necessarily go with that of covenant sacrifice. Rather, as in Mark, it concerns, on the first level, the violent death of the cross, a non-ritual form of expiation by which the final *berîth* is set up and established in power.

2. *The Actions*

Of crucial importance is the fact that Jesus reveals through his *actions* at the last supper that this new order of salvation will assert itself in this world and is not simply reserved for the future parousia. This disclosure is brought to full expression in the use which Jesus makes of bread and wine. Jesus compares himself to bread and wine by terms which in the Greek text are rendered *soma* and *haima:* body and blood. The word body, used in B.C. and A.D. Greek writings as well as in post-biblical Hebrew and Aramaic, under Hellenistic influence, to refer to body in contrast to soul, also was employed to designate the whole person. This use is in keeping with the Semitic anthropology which looks on man as "flesh". The use of the term blood, "the substance of life" for the Hebrew, for the whole person was likewise familiar to the Jews of this period. Normally Jesus would have used the more common expression "to give his life" (literally: soul), as in Mark 10, 45b, where the service of Jesus is interpreted as fulfillment of the role of the Servant of Yahweh. However, the term body allows for a closer connection with bread. Likewise the term blood allows for a closer link with wine and points to the violent death. It is doubtful that the original bread saying would be more correctly translated by *sarx* (flesh). This is done in John 6, 51-56, with the result that the twin concept, flesh-blood, used to designate the components of a sacrificial animal after it had been killed, comes into play. This development seems to have been influenced by later theological reflection which formally envisions Jesus' death as antitype of the Old Testament sacrifices. At least the translators of the original saying show no awareness that Jesus was applying to himself this sacrificial twin concept. Furthermore, the two terms, body (flesh) and blood, were not closely enough linked at the last supper to allow this interpretation. The cup saying took place after the meal as the expression "after supper" indicates in 1 Corinthians 11, 25. Consequently both sayings are to be interpreted as self-contained units. By way of climactic parallelism, Jesus expressed in a more dramatic way in the cup saying what was revealed in the bread saying.

The context in which Jesus spoke reveals the point of the comparison between body-bread and wine-blood. Having taken bread, he pronounced the usual blessing, broke the bread and gave it to the disciples. By eating this bread they believed, as pious Jews, that they received a personal share in the blessing which had been spoken. Hence it was a holy action, observed in silence and undertaken as soon as the one who had pronounced the blessing began to eat. However, on this occasion Jesus acts differently. Instead of immediately eating, he speaks: "Take; this is my body which is given for many." At the end of the meal Jesus acts in a similar way. Having spoken the final blessing over the cup, instead of drinking and handing the cup to the others in silence, he again speaks as he gives the cup to the disciple next to him: "This is my blood of the covenant, which is shed for many."

The point of the comparison lies in the act of mediation. By this bread and wine, now identified with his body and blood, Jesus mediates to the disciples not merely a share in the table blessing but more properly a share in the blessings derived from his "given body" and "shed blood": freedom from the power of sin and a new covenant union with God. We should, in this connection, speak of a kind of sacramental presence of Jesus under the forms of bread and wine at the last supper which makes the eating of this consecrated bread and the drinking of accounts record that Jesus actually said: "Do this in remem-tion "by anticipation". However, we should not confuse this sacramental presence with that reserved for the period after the resurrection when the glorified Lord, no longer bound by the limitations of space and time, comes to his own under the forms of bread and wine.

All the accounts of institution make clear that Jesus intended this rite of the bread and cup to be repeated. The Paul/Luke accounts record that Jesus actually said: "Do this in remembrance of me." This command, which may be an authentic saying of Jesus, refers to the repetition of the essential ritual gestures and words which are said to have a memorial function. We can safely conjecture that the specific Jewish concept of "ritual memorial of the saving works of God" is operative here. This would mean that the eucharist falls into the class of memorial rites of which the passover feast was the type par excellence. By the cultic repetition of the saving events of the Exodus at the passover, the pious Jews were convinced that they encountered Yahweh's saving activity in a special way. Seen from this viewpoint the eucharist is not merely intended as the occasion for the subjective recall by the believers of the crucial events of Jesus' life. Rather they are to recall, in the sense of participate in, the reenactment of the last supper as a means of personal encounter with the Kyrios and the power of his redemptive work.

II
EASTER MEALS

On the day of the resurrection Jesus ate with the disciples at Emmaus and again participated in a meal in the cenacle with the eleven and others gathered with them (Lk. 24, 30-31, 36-43). The unusually detailed description of the common introductory rite of the meal at Emmaus is reminiscent of the description found in the account of institution: "He took the bread and blessed, and broke it, and gave it to them" (Lk. 24, 30). The term employed for this action, "the breaking of the bread" (Lk. 24, 35), is the earliest designation of the Lord's supper. This eucharistic coloring has led some authors to equate this Easter meal with the eucharist. This interpretation, however, does not seem to be well supported. This meal belongs to the transitory period, however brief, between Jesus' death-glorification and the coming of the Spirit. According to Luke, *after* eating with the disciples Jesus enjoined them to prepare for the decisive experience of being "clothed with power from on high" (24, 49). Only with the Pentecostal event is the effective inauguration of the kingdom in its ecclesial dimension realized (Acts 1, 8; 2, 1-4), and so the banquet of the kingdom: the eucharist. Hence, it is difficult to imagine that Luke viewed this Easter meal as the first eucharist of the Church.

The fact that the risen Lord eats with the disciples who had forsaken him indicates that they are readmitted to his table fellowship: it is a visible sign of forgiveness. These meals also provide a basis for faith in the resurrection. From the remark of Acts 10, 41 we discover how intimately the thought of the resurrection was connected with the Easter meals: "who ate and drank with him after he rose from the dead." Finally, they served as a bridge between the meals of the public life and the post-Easter meals with the invisible Kyrios.

The Easter meals made a tremendous impression on the disciples. After Pentecost they could not come together for a meal without the conviction that the Kyrios would reveal himself. In these later meals they experienced his presence in the pure eschatological joy and other concrete manifestations of the Spirit such as prophecy and ecstatic utterances (1 Cor. 12, 14), but especially in the "breaking of the bread".

III
COMMUNAL MEALS OF THE EARLIEST COMMUNITY

In the communal meals of the primitive Church, the introductory rite of the breaking of the bread had taken on a new meaning because now it was done at the command of Christ and after his example at the last supper. In the earliest period it appears to have retained its usual place and was separated from the blessing of the cup by a meal. Quite naturally, then, the term "breaking of the bread" was used to describe the whole Lord's supper by way of synecdoche (Acts 2, 42. 46; 20, 7, 11).

Accounts of the post-Easter meals are found in Acts 2, 42, 46-47a. The older source used by Luke in constructing this passage seems to have contained the essentials of vv. 46-47a, while v. 42

is secondary.[2] The latter text reads: "They were devoting themselves to the teaching of the apostles and to the *koinonia*, to the breaking of the bread and to prayers." This may be a description of the actual sequence of an early service in which the rite of the cup and bread were already joined together at the end of the meal: (1) teaching of the apostles; (2) *koinonia:* meal of fellowship; (3) breaking of the bread: the phrase now referring only to the rite of the cup and bread; (4) solemn prayers. The text of Acts 2, 46-47a should read: "And daily they attended together in the temple and broke the bread at home; they took the food with joy and simplicity of heart, praising God and standing in favor with all the people." [3] We learn from this pericope that visits to the temple and the "breaking of the bread" were daily events. The characteristic tone of the meal was joy and the food was taken with "simplicity of heart", i.e., no secondary motive diverted the attention of the participants from "praising God".

The source of joy was the expectation of the imminent coming of the kingdom and the awareness of the presence of the Kyrios. The expectation of the final coming of the Kyrios caused the spontaneous outcry *"Maranatha"* (Our Lord, come!), which became a characteristic prayer of the Lord's supper and was retained in the Aramaic form even in the Hellenistic churches (1 Cor. 16, 22). Objectively this formula could be translated in the indicative sense (our Lord is coming.), but this is unlikely. Considering the lively expectation of the parousia, we are inclined to think it was used with reference to this at least in the beginning. Afterward it may also have become a specific prayer of petition for the presence of the Kyrios at the meal: a primitive type of epiclesis.

This joy had a soteriological character based on the awareness of sharing in the fruits of Christ's redemptive death. Seen in the brilliance of the resurrection, this death was viewed as part of the

---

[2] Cf. A. B. Du Toit, *Des Aspekt der Freude im urchristlichen Abendmahl* (Winterthur, 1965), pp. 105-112.
[3] *Ibid.*, p. 106.

one joyous saving event in which Jesus fulfilled the role of the Servant whose humiliation served as pathway to his exaltation and the reconciliation of men with God (Is. 53, 10-12). This Ebed Yahweh Christology is the most ancient solution given to the death of Jesus in the earliest preaching of Acts (3, 13-14; 8, 32-35, etc.). On this grounds alone it would be correct to assume that this theme was introduced into the Lord's supper very early. Moreover, we have every reason to suppose that it was explicitly linked to the "breaking of the bread". In the words of institution, Jesus reveals his role as Servant and the liturgical accounts of institution, removing secondary forms, go back at least to the first ten years after the death of Jesus.

In the beginning it is probable that a formal distinction between the general presence and the special presence of the Kyrios related to the bread and wine was not made. The form of the meal in which the rite of the bread and cup were separated by the agape would tend to encourage this outlook. However, within the first ten years these two rites were joined together and, in general, probably placed at the end of the meal. The symmetrical style of the accounts indicates that they formed literary units recited at one time. The end of the meal was chosen since, according to Jewish custom, at this point the most solemn prayer was recited and hymns sung. Direct evidence for the position of the eucharist at the close of the meal is found in 1 Corinthians 11, 21. 33, where Paul states that the meal did not begin in common. This rearrangement shows that the saving presence of the Kyrios is ascribed in a special way to the rite of the bread and cup. This belief is expressed by the pre-Pauline formula found in 1 Corinthians 10, 16.

This communal meal was celebrated in the evening when the principal meal was normally taken. If our interpretation of Acts 2, 46 is correct, it was a daily occurrence at first. The reference to a Sunday eucharist in Acts 20, 7-11 may indicate what afterward became normative. The choice of Sunday may have been dictated by the fact that Christ rose from the dead and ate with the disciples on that day. As might be expected the joy of the participants expressed itself in typical Jewish fashion by the singing of hymns and psalms. The meal always involved the ministry of the word (Acts 2, 42; 20, 7-11). Finally, there was the service of love directed toward the needy brethren. Acts 6, 2 refers to serving the poor at table. Since a division into meals for poor Christians and others involving the "breaking of the bread" is improbable, we must assume that this ministry took place in the daily agape-eucharist. Only when the eucharist was stripped of its link with the agape was there need of other meals for the poor. This service of the needy was considered a very important task which the apostles themselves did not understand only because of the more pressing needs of "preaching the word of God" (Acts 6, 2, 4).

A discussion of the post-Easter meals would not be complete without reference to the interpretation given to the miraculous feedings of Jesus by the primitive Church.[4] Jesus is presented as the new Moses who feeds the hungry crowd in the desert place. The messianic coloring, due to the Exodus motif, brings these accounts into harmony with the pronounced eschatological character of the earliest Lord's supper. It may have the result of a conscious effort to connect these meals with the eucharist. A eucharistic coloring of both miracles in Matthew is certain. The earlier forms of the accounts in Mark show an interesting variation in the key verses for a eucharistic reference. Instead of reading, "He blessed and broke the bread" (Mk. 6, 41), the second account states: "Having given thanks, he broke them" (Mk. 8, 6). This change brings the text more into conformity with Mark's account of institution (Mk. 14, 22), but it exactly parallels the Pauline account of 1 Corinthians 11, 24. Since Mark should have used "having blessed" (*eulogēsas*) instead of the Pauline "having given thanks" (*eucharistēsas*), we can conclude that this eucharistic coloring was borrowed by Mark from an earlier tradition. Both accounts are probably variants of one miracle story: one originating in a Palestinian, the other in a Hellen-

[4] Mt. 14, 13-21; 15, 32-39; Mk. 6, 31-44; 8, 1-11; Lk. 9, 10-17; Jn. 6, 1-15.

istic milieu. The relationship between Mark 14, 22, a Judeo-Christian account of institution, and the first feeding miracle, and between 1 Corinthians 11, 24, a Hellenistic account of institution, and the second feeding miracle, shows this.

We may assume that the earliest Christians, who recognized the eschatological significance of the meals of Jesus' public life, attributed to the feeding miracles the same meaning and, seeing in them the anticipation of the eucharistic meal of the Church, explicitly interpreted them as such. These accounts fall into the class of kerygmatic miracle stories. Transformed by theological reflection, they present a confession of faith in the meaning of the eucharist: Just as Jesus, the new Moses fed the hungry crowd in the desert place with bread, so now, in the meal of the Church, the resurrected Lord is present feeding his followers with the bread "which endures to eternal life" (Jn. 6, 27).

Luc Dequeker/*Mechelen, Belgium*
Willem Zuidema/*Brussels, Belgium*

The Eucharist and
St. Paul (1 Cor. 11, 17-34)

We cannot discuss St. Paul's view of the Lord's supper without considering the pre-Pauline messianic expectations which Paul saw realized in the celebration of this meal. Nor can we discuss the Lord's supper and the eucharist without describing the messianic reality (peace and redemption) which is expressed therein.

Although the term "messianic supper" is not used in the New Testament, we have sufficient evidence to conclude that Jesus did regard the last supper as such, and that the nascent messianic community celebrated it as such. Israel commemorated the exodus from Egypt in the paschal meal; in celebrating this meal, she participated in the deliverance of God's People. In like manner, the messianic community commemorated Christ's exodus on the cross (Lk. 9, 31); in celebrating the eucharist, it proclaimed the messianic peace and redemption which had now become a tangible reality.

"Do this in remembrance of me . . . as often as you shall eat this bread and drink the cup, you proclaim the death of the Lord" (1 Cor. 11, 24-26). Fully aware of the definitive, eschatological significance of his action, Jesus transformed the paschal meal (*seder*), which he celebrated with his disciples on the eve of his propitiatory death, into a messianic supper. Henceforth his

48

disciples would commemorate the exodus par excellence, the messianic deliverance. "For I myself have received from the Lord what I also delivered to you . . ." (1 Cor. 11, 23).

In his letter to the Corinthians, Paul contrasts the "Lord's supper" with their gatherings, where "each one takes first his own supper, and one is hungry and another drinks too much" (1 Cor. 11, 20-21). The "Lord's supper" is one where we commemorate the messianic act of salvation, where the Lord is present with his peace, where the messianic deliverance is rendered present. The egotism of many Christians in Corinth, however, was making it impossible to celebrate the Lord's supper in the community of God (1 Cor. 11, 22).

At the Lord's supper, everyone ate the one bread. Because the bread was one, it made the community one body, the body of Christ (1 Cor. 10, 16-17); in short, it turned the community into a messianic body. Every instance of egotism and division was reprehensible because it damaged the reality of Christ and his body, because it hindered the process of building up Christ's body to its full measure (Eph. 2, 19-22; 4, 16).

I

Messianic Expectations

The backdrop for Paul's remarks on the body of Christ, peace and the messianic meal is the messianic expectations of the Jewish nation.[1] It is clear that this messianic longing, as evidenced in the gospels and Paul's epistles, was not uniform. On the whole, we can distinguish three basic outlooks on messianism: prophetic messianism, apocalyptic messianism and rabbinic messianism.

The prophetic messianism we find in Isaiah was particularly important for St. Paul, especially with regard to the place of the "nations" (i.e., the gentiles) in this salvation. Two aspects deserve special stress: the messianic peace (Is. 2, 1-5) and the

---

[1] We use the term "messianic" in its broadest sense here.

messianic banquet (Is. 25, 6-12).[2] They had a dominant place in Paul's own convictions.

Messianic peace is the peace which the Messiah, the Anointed One, will inaugurate in the world at the end of time. No longer will there be conflict between Israel, God's chosen people, and "the nations" (Is. 2, 4). The situation will be radically different. "In days to come, the mountain of the Lord's house shall be established as the highest mountain and raised above the hills. All nations shall stream toward it. Many people shall come and say: 'Come, let us climb the Lord's mountain, to the house of the God of Jacob, that he may instruct us in his ways, and we may walk in his paths'" (Is. 2, 2-3).

In messianic times, Israel will remain at the center of God's election: "For from Sion shall go forth instruction, and the word of the Lord from Jerusalem" (Is. 2, 3). But the nations of non-Jews, the gentiles, will no longer be excluded; they will ascend to Jerusalem to be instructed by the God of Israel (see also Is. 60 and 62, Zech. 14, 12). What is more, they will be able to parti-cipate in the messianic meal that celebrates Israel's definitive deliverance (Is. 25, 9): "On the mountain the Lord of hosts will provide *for all peoples* a feast of rich food . . . On the mountain he will destroy the veil that veils all peoples, the web that is woven over all nations . . ." (Is. 25, 6-7).

Exodus 12, 48 stipulates that no uncircumcised person may participate in the paschal meal; in short, all non-Jews are ex-cluded. In the rabbinical writings we find this same strict condi-tion governing participation in the messianic meal. The just among the nations (the *chasside-ha-olam*) can participate fully in the feast only if they are circumcised and become Jews. In Isaiah, by contrast, we no longer find any trace of the precept.

Paul, in his turn, comes out and says that the uncircumcised faithful share fully in the messianic salvation brought by Jesus.

---

[2] The question of attributing Isaiah 25 to the prophet is not at issue here. Whatever the case may be, it is clear that this image is employed in the prophetic vocabulary and is pre-apocalyptic.

Paul justifies his stance by arguing that the uncircumcised who observe the precepts of the law are circumcised in God's eyes; for authentic circumcision is a matter of the heart (Rom. 2, 26-29; compare Rom. 2, 13 and Col. 2, 11ff).

Even as early as the book of Deuteronomy we find the sacred author reacting against the emphasis on physical circumcision (Dt. 10, 16; 30, 6); it is not on a par with circumcision of the heart. In an analogous context we find Jeremiah comparing Israel with the gentiles and protesting against the nationalistic outlook which equates salvation with physical circumcision (Jer. 4, 4; 9, 24ff).

Paul formulates his own *halakha* [3] on the basis of Jeremiah's protestation. He concludes that circumcision of the heart has the same value for uncircumcised peoples as bodily circumcision has for the Jews. Bodily circumcision does retain its value for the Jews (Rom. 3, 1-3; Acts 16, 3), however, so long as it is tied up with observance of the law (Rom. 2, 25).

II
MESSIANIC PEACE

Here we can readily see that Paul's formulas were, to a large extent, the product of a lively theological and juridical debate with his contemporaries and his fellow Jews. He argued with them over the meaning of the messianic reality, in which both circumcised and uncircumcised participated. "For he himself is our *peace*, he it is who has made both one, and has broken down the intervening wall . . . that of the two he might create in himself one new man . . ." (Eph. 2, 14-15).

The concept of peace (i.e., messianic peace) plays a very important role in the theology of St. Paul. Here, as in Isaiah, it refers to peace between Israel and the nations. Those who were

---

[3] "halakha": a "juridical" interpretation of scripture relating to rules of conduct.

far away have drawn close in Jesus Christ. Now they share salvation in the one body of the Messiah. We must pay close attention to Paul's treatment of messianic peace and Jew-gentile relations, because he sees the eucharistic celebration as the realization and the expression of the one body constituted by Jesus the Messiah.

On the basis of Isaiah 57, 19 and 52, 7, Paul talks to the Ephesians about those who were once *far off* and who have now come *near* (Eph. 2, 13. 17-18). The Jewish rabbis used the same words with regard to proselytes. The gentiles were *far off*, the Jews were *near*. To accept a non-Jew as a proselyte was to "bring him near".[4]

Paul contradicts this view. He says that the "gentiles" [5] have been brought *near* through the blood of the Messiah,[6] without circumcision (Eph. 2, 13). "Therefore, you are now no longer strangers and foreigners, but you are citizens with the saints and members of God's household" (Eph. 2, 19). The peace effected by the Messiah means that the physically uncircumcised are no longer excluded from Israel's heritage. They have become fellow citizens with the saints, and full members of God's nation. They are now part of the People of God.[7]

The Messiah has effected peace by destroying the hostility between Jew and gentile. This hostility resulted from the age-old insistence on bodily circumcision. By insisting on this circumcision, Israel had kept the nations "far" from the salvation she was supposed to bring to them. Instead of being a light to the nations, instead of bringing salvation to the ends of the earth (Is. 42, 4. 6-7; 49, 6), her law became a barrier between Israel and the world.

---

[4] Strack-Billerbeck, III, 585ff.

[5] "Gentiles", as used in Saint Paul, should always be interpreted in the ethnic connotation of "non-Jew, uncircumcised". The gentiles to whom St. Paul addressed himself were, for the most part, God-fearing people who had abandoned polytheism and now imbibed the spiritual atmosphere of the synagogue. But they had not been circumcised, so they were not Jews.

[6] *en tō haimati tou Christou:* whenever Paul uses the article in speaking of Christ, we can translate it as "the Messiah".

[7] Comp. Ex. 19, 6; 1 Pt. 2, 4-10.

Is the notion of "peace" present in Paul's discussion of the eucharist (1 Cor. 11, 17-34)? "When you meet together, it is no longer possible to eat the Lord's supper" (1 Cor. 11, 20). The tensions and disputes in the Corinthian community (1 Cor. 1, 10-12; 3, 3) are in direct opposition to the eucharist, to the messianic feast they are supposed to be celebrating. The eucharist should be a sign of unity. At the Lord's supper the one body of Christ should be respected; in other words, the messianic reality should be visible. "For he who eats and drinks unworthily, without distinguishing the body, eats and drinks judgment to himself" (1 Cor. 11, 29). "Because the bread is one, we though many, are one body, all of us who partake of the one bread" (1 Cor. 10, 17).

We have no clear information about the tensions prevailing in Corinth. Whatever they were, they were dividing Christ (1 Cor. 1, 13) and casting aspersions on the community of God (1 Cor. 11, 22). It is worth noting that in this overall context Paul talks about conflict between the Greeks and the Jews: "The Jews ask for signs, and the Greeks look for wisdom" (1 Cor. 1, 22).

Paul has no desire to get involved in factionalism, so he does not take sides. He has only one interest: "We, for our part, preach a crucified Christ—to the Jews indeed a stumbling block and to the gentiles foolishness—but to those who are called, both Jews and Greeks, Christ, the power of God and the wisdom of God" (1 Cor. 1, 23-24).

III
THE NEW COVENANT

To correctly interpret Paul's text on the eucharist (1 Cor. 11, 23-29), we must take serious account of the immediate context. In response to the division in the community, Paul talks about the eucharist, about the tradition he received from the Lord. The celebration of the eucharist is a guarantee of the unity of God's

People.[8] If a person celebrates the eucharistic meal without respecting the unity of Christ's body, he thereby condemns himself.

The unity of God's People is sealed by Christ's blood: "This cup is the new covenant in my blood" (1 Cor. 11, 25). Thanks to the blood of the Messiah, those "who were once afar off have been brought near" (Eph. 2, 13). The blood of Christ is the blood of propitiation that makes possible the community of one body.

Blood plays an important role in the biblical theology of the covenant. The Israelite was not allowed to nourish himself on blood because blood contains the life-giving force in man and animals, and life belongs to God. Blood could only be used in a propitiatory sacrifice. It is to be sprinkled on the altar, "for the life of the creature is in the blood . . . it is the blood which as the life makes atonement" (Lev. 17, 11).

Blood also played a role in the establishment of the covenant. After Moses had read the book of the covenant to the people, he took the blood of the holocaust victims and sprinkled it on them saying: "Behold the blood of the covenant which the Lord has made with you on the basis of all these regulations" (Ex. 24, 8). The community of blood expresses the covenant community between God and his people. Whenever the covenant is broken by his people's infidelity, it is restored by the blood of propitiation (Lev. 16).

In their account of the institution of the eucharist, Luke and Paul speak about the *new covenant in my blood* (Lk. 22, 20; 1 Cor. 11, 25). Matthew and Mark echo the formula of Exodus 24, 8: *the blood of the covenant* (Mt. 26, 28; Mk. 14, 24). The terminology of Paul and Luke echoes Jeremiah's theme of the new covenant (Jer. 31, 31-34).

"The days are coming, says the Lord, when I will make a new covenant with the house of Israel and the house of Judah" (Jer. 31, 31). The prophet indicates that God will fashion a new cove-

---

[8] *ekklēsia:* in St. Paul it signifies more than simply "church" or "community"; it is the community of those who have been called and who do reply to God's call. It often has the same sense as "People of God".

nant because the Israelites have broken his old covenant with their forefathers. In the new covenant, God will engrave his law in man's heart: "I will place my law within them, and write it upon their hearts; I will be their God, and they shall be my people" (Jer. 31, 33; cf. Rom 2, 15).[9]

The people's heart of stone, disobedient and unfaithful, is replaced with a heart of flesh—i.e., a new heart and a new spirit that will never again break God's age-old covenant with Israel's forefathers (Ez. 36, 26-28). "All, from least to greatest, shall know me, says the Lord; for I will forgive their evildoing and remember their sin no more" (Jer. 31, 34).

We can say that the blood indicated the separation of Jew from gentile. In the *Mishna* we read that the admission of a proselyte is not complete until the altar is sprinkled with the blood of his holocaust.[10] That, according to St. Paul, is precisely what has been accomplished by the blood of Jesus. The blood of the Messiah has brought near those who were far off. The blood of the new covenant makes atonement for all, for both Jews and gentiles, who are now brought together in the same covenant. God has brought peace and reconciled all things in heaven and on earth through the blood poured out on the cross (Col. 1, 20).

Thus the notion of the covenant is present in the celebration of the eucharistic meal. On the basis of the direct and indirect allusions to Exodus 24, 8 (by Matthew/Mark and Paul/Luke respectively), we can say that the verb *ek-chunnomenon* ("shed", "pour out") alludes to two things. It alludes to Moses' sprinkling of the people at the ratification of the covenant, and it also alludes to the blood sprinkled on the altar during the atonement rites (Exodus and Leviticus). The Hebrew text uses the same term (*zrq*) for both aspersions.

In the celebration of the Lord's supper, this same aspersion is rendered present; it ratifies the covenant and remits sins. "This cup is the new covenant in my blood; do this as often as you

[9] See Jer. 31, 36-37, and compare with Rom. 11, 28 (9, 4). Jer. 31, 33-34 is cited in Rom. 11, 27.
[10] *Keritot* 2, 1.

drink it, in remembrance of me" (1 Cor. 11, 25). The chalice of the eucharist is communion in the blood of Christ (1 Cor. 10, 16). In other words, the blood of the Messiah effects the restoration of the covenant community in which non-Jews now participate. A new *koinonia* (Acts 2, 42!) is established; it is the community of the new covenant, the community of the Messiah's blood.

In Paul's account of the Lord's supper, we come across one formula several times: *the body of Christ*. "This is my body which shall be given up for you" (1 Cor. 11, 24); "whosoever eats this bread or drinks the cup of the Lord unworthily will be guilty of the body and the blood of the Lord (1 Cor. 11, 27; see 1 Cor. 11, 29 also). The first expression (1 Cor. 11, 24), *to sōma to hyper hymōn,* is part of the terminology of sacrifice.

On the cross Jesus gave his life for men, putting himself in their place. His physical death as the sacrificial victim signifies atonement for the whole world. The body of the crucified Christ is like the covering on the ark of the covenant that is sprinkled with the blood of atonement (Lev. 16). It is no longer hidden from the eyes of the profane by the temple veil.[11] It is now exposed openly and accessible to all, both Jews and non-Jews: ". . . Christ Jesus, whom God has set forth as a propitiation by his blood through faith . . ." (Rom 3, 25).[12]

In the Lord's supper, the propitiatory death of Christ (i.e., the messianic redemption on Golgotha) is made present, just as the deliverance from Egypt and the Sinai covenant had been rendered truly present in the Jewish pasch. Celebrating Israel's pasch and commemorating her deliverance, the Jew was delivered from Egypt.[13] And so it is with the Lord's supper: "This is my body, which is being given for you; do this in remembrance

---

[11] Lev. 16, 16; Mt. 27, 51; Heb. 9, 3. The profane are the gentiles; the Jewish people have access to the "holy of holies" through their priests.

[12] Remember the context in which Rom. 3, 25 is spoken: "the justice of God through faith in Jesus Christ upon all who believe. *For there is no distinction . . .*" (v. 22).

[13] This "celebration and commemoration" of the Jewish pasch are what one could call a "sacramental" act or, if you will, a "sacred" act: a holy

of me" (Lk. 22, 19; 1 Cor. 11, 24). The bread and wine of the Lord's supper, and the proclamation of his death, make present Christ's physical body and blood. They make visible the deliverance of Golgotha: "For as often as you shall eat this bread and drink the cup, you proclaim the death of the Lord, until he comes" (1 Cor. 11, 26).

St. Paul does not use the term, "body of Christ", solely to refer to Christ's physical body on the cross. He also uses it in a figurative sense when he speaks of the meal. The expression, *to sōma tou christou*, is applied to the community in the context of the eucharist. This is clear from 1 Corinthians 10, 17: "Because the bread is one, we though many, are one body, all of us who partake of the one bread." [14]

Paul insists on the unity of the Church, on the entente between Jews and gentiles; it is threatened by the practice of sacrificing to idols, a practice which shocked Christians of Jewish lineage. The unity of the community must be preserved at all cost because Christians form a single body in sharing the same bread. They share in the body of the Messiah as Paul points out in 1 Corinthians 10, 16. And the connection between verse 16 and verse 17 indicates that the *sōma tou christou* of verse 16 also refers to the community, to the one body formed and fashioned by the Messiah. The community is the body of the Messiah; it is the "messianic" body in which is effected the messianic peace (i.e., unity) and redemption.

Paul picks up this theme at several points in his letters. We find it in the texts where he describes the one body made up of many members (Rom. 12, 5; 1 Cor. 12, 12). But we also find it when he describes the unity and reality of the People of God in terms of "his body" or "the body of Christ" (1 Cor. 12, 27; Eph. 1, 23; 4, 12; Col. 1, 24; 2, 17).

---

communion meal tied up with a recital of the deliverance and exodus from Egypt. "Word and element" render this deliverance present. Here we probably have one of the most ancient cultic acts of the Bible. Cf. Schurmann in this volume.

[14] Cf. J. J. Meuzelaar, *Der Leib des Messias: Eine exegetische Studie über den Gedanken vom Leib Christi in den Paulusbriefen* (Assen, 1961).

In the one messianic body there is no longer any opposition between Jews and Greeks, slaves and freemen (1 Cor. 12, 13), male and female (Gal. 3, 28). Now Paul has no desire whatsoever to glaze over the difference between man and woman, rich and poor, or even Jew and gentile. But the messianic body should be the place where all, in their diversity, serve the Lord (1 Cor. 12, 14 ff).

Thus the term *sōma tou christou* in St. Paul indicates *the messianic reality* which Christ effects in the world. It is with good reason that one translates the *sōma tou christou* of Colossians 2, 17 as "the reality (or substance) of Christ" whose shadow had been glimpsed in an earlier day.

Paul uses the term "body", first and foremost, to explain the significance of Christ's coming and the messianic reality for human interrelationships—particularly for relations between those (near) who already belonged to the body and those (far off) who now are grafted onto it (Eph. 3, 6).

The Church can rightfully be called an *ekklēsia;* she truly is the body of Christ, to the extent that she incarnates the messianic reality and expresses the unity of God's People. The body of Christ must be "built up" (Eph. 4, 12).

The *ekklēsia* must grow into the full measure of Christ, "who is the head" (Eph. 4, 15). In Christ we find the fullness (Col. 1, 19) which must also be attained in the Church. The Messiah is the first, the beginning, the firstborn [15] who comprises the whole. The head, the Messiah, represents the whole *ekklēsia*.[16]

By referring to the community as the body of the Messiah, Paul indicates the moral and practical consequences of the messianic peace and redemption manifested in Jesus of Nazareth. The metaphor of the "body" arose in extra-biblical philosophy,

[15] "Head" (Hebrew: *r's*) signifies the first, the beginning, the best, which contains the whole.

[16] We know that the image of the body, which Paul uses to designate the Church, and the title "head", which he gives to Christ, are of diverse origin and also employed separately by Paul. Thus Paul never says that Christ is the head of the body; he is the head of the community which is his body (Eph. 1, 22; 5, 23; Col. 1, 18; cf. J. J. Meuzelaar, *op. cit.*, pp. 122-23).

but it was familiar to post-biblical Judaism. Paul used it to define, in the most concrete terms possible, the messianic reality which had come about through Christ's death and which was realized in the celebration of the eucharist.

So long as Christians remain divided, so long as they remain a stumbling block for world peace, they merit Paul's words of reproach. They eat the bread and drink the cup unworthily; they are "guilty of the body and the blood of the Lord" (1 Cor. 11, 27).

Jean Giblet/*Heverlee, Belgium*

The Eucharist in
St. John's Gospel (John 6)

In all the evangelical traditions, the multiplication of the loaves holds an important place. It represents a high point in the manifestation of Jesus' messianic power and a critical juncture in the decision for or against faith.[1]

Like the synoptics, John relates Christ's walking on the water here also. But he follows this account with a long discourse by Jesus on the "bread from heaven". In recent times there have been many studies which have attempted to give a detailed analysis of this discourse and its structure.[2] There is, in particular, the research of P. Borgen which has shed light on the midrashic structure of the discourse. After a preamble (6, 26-30), the "discourse" seeks to elucidate a passage in Scripture: "Bread from heaven he gave them to eat" (6, 31; Ps. 78, 24; Ex. 16, 4). Jesus adapts this text (6, 32ff.) and then develops his explanation of it (6, 34-40). This is followed by an exegetical debate (6, 41-48), and it concludes with a eucharistic homily which ties together the various themes already explicitated (6, 49-58).[3]

---

[1] Cf. Mk. 6, 32-44; 8, 1-10; Mt. 14, 13-21; 15, 32-39; Lk. 9, 10-17. For a survey of recent study see H. Lessig, *Die Abendmahlsprobleme im Lichte der neutest. Forschung seit 1900* (Bonn, 1933); R. Brown, *The Gospel According to John* (New York, 1966), I, pp. 303f.

[2] R. Brown, *ibid.*, pp. 293f.

[3] P. Borgen, "Observations on the Midrashic Character of John 6," in *ZNW* 54 (1963), pp. 232-40.

The majority of recent commentators agree that there is an explicit eucharistic sense in the last section, at least from 6, 51c or 6, 52.[4] But some of them felt obliged to attribute the redaction to the hand of an editor who was anxious to harmonize John's teaching with the sacramental doctrine of the Church as a whole. However, the studies of E. Ruckstuhl have shown that the section possesses several typically Johannine traits; and E. Schweizer, abandoning the thesis of inauthenticity which he had held for a long time, now points out that it is no longer possible to challenge the authenticity of the text on the basis of literary devices.[5]

Now even if it is true that there are some new notions and ideas here, it cannot be shown that they are in opposition to the overall orientation of Johannine thought.[6] Here, however, I should like to show that they flow naturally from the perspectives opened up by the preceding developments, and that they fit easily into the total context of John's thought.

Eschatological Nourishment

John begins by relating the story of the multiplication of the loaves. A crowd follows Jesus across the sea, and they are fed to satiety with loaves of bread. The miracle enkindles the enthusiasm of the crowd, who see Jesus as "the prophet who is to come into the world", and who try to make him king. Immediately we are in an atmosphere of messianic exaltation, and the evocation of a new Exodus comes all too easily.

Even more explicitly than in the synoptics, however, Jesus breaks off the mood and retreats to the solitude of a mountain.

[4] In recent times several authors have held a purely metaphorical interpretation of the section: B. Weiss (1893), H. Odeberg (1929), A. Schlatter (1930), H. Strathmann (1951).

[5] E. Ruckstuhl, *Die literarische Einheit des Johannesevangeliums* (Freiburg S., 1951), pp. 220ff.; E. Schweizer, "Das johanneische Zeugnis vom Herrenmahl," in *EvTh* 12 (1952/53), pp. 341ff.; J. Jeremias, "Joh. 6, 51c-58: redaktionell?" in *ZNW* 44 (1952/53), pp. 256f.

[6] R. Bultmann, *Das Evangelium nach Johannes* (Göttingen, 1941), pp. 161f, 174-77. He rejects its authenticity in the light of his picture of Johannine eschatology. Cf. G. Bornkamm, "Die eucharistische Rede im Johannesevangelium," in *ZNW* 47 (1956), pp. 161-70.

His real work is on another level, and it must follow a different road. When he comes to his disciples on the water that night, he enlightens them by saying "It is I" (i.e. I am). In the context of the fourth gospel, this remark is undoubtedly an evocation of the formula in Exodus, which designates God.[7] The discourse which follows (6, 22ff.) tries to show that we must get beyond first-impression interpretations of the miracle-sign and eventually arrive at the divine nature of Jesus.

The ensuing dialogue immediately reveals the incomprehension of the very people who had hailed Jesus as the Messiah. They are trying to fit him into the image which they themselves had fashioned. They do not understand the real import of the "sign" (6, 26), and they are looking for material advantages only.

Jesus, however, asserts that there is a radical difference between this perishable food and the food "which endures unto life everlasting which the Son of Man will give you" (6, 27). Food gives life; it is the principle of life. And just as the evangelist makes a clear distinction between life according to the flesh and life according to the Spirit, so he makes a clear distinction between two types of nourishment.[8] Jesus announces a new order of existence which finds its origin and its growth in God, and he gives men the possibility of entering this new order.

The significance of mentioning the title, Son of Man, in this context will be discussed later. But first we must consider the import of various expressions that tie in with "the food . . . that endures unto life everlasting".

This expression evokes, first of all, the wisdom literature of the Old Testament. Wisdom has built her house and set her table for all. "To the senseless man she says: 'Come, eat of my bread, and

---

[7] Cf. D. Daube, The "I am" of the Messianic Presence in the NT and Rabbinic Judaism (London, 1956), pp. 325ff.; H. Zimmerman, "Das absolute 'Ego eimi' als die neutestamentliche Offenbarungsformel," in BZ 4 (1960), pp. 54-69; 266-76; R. Brown, op. cit., pp. 533-38.

[8] Cf. 3, 3-6; 4, 10-15; cf. E. Percy, Untersuchungen über den Ursprung der johanneischen Theologie (Lund, 1939), pp. 13ff.; F. Mussner, Zoē: Die Anschauung vom 'Leben' im vierten Evangelium (Munich, 1952), pp. 128ff.

drink of the wine I have mingled' " (Prov. 9, 5). The point here concerns specific teachings that will insure authentic life to those who live by them.

This same theme is picked up often in the sapiential literature: "Come to me, you who desire me, and fill yourselves with my produce . . . Those who eat me will still be hungry, and those who drink me will still be thirsty. He who obeys me will not be put to shame" (Sir. 24, 19ff.). The wisdom of God is hypostatized, as it were; her teachings are transmitted by tradition and the lessons of the sages, and only those who accept and practice them will know authentic life. This is the context in which the image of food appears.[9]

Recent criticism has shed light on the influence of sapiential literary style on the language of John.[10] In John the imagery is deepened considerably, of course. Wisdom is identified with Christ, the Logos who was made flesh [11] and who gives those who believe in him the chance to become children of God. But one can transpose the sapiential formulas to the food which gives eschatological life.[12] Thus, right from the start of John 6 we find a contrast between the food that perishes (or allows men to perish) and the food that endures unto life everlasting.

This image summons up another: the image of the new manna. Jewish tradition, as we know, told how Yahweh had nourished his people day after day during their sojourn in the desert (Ex. 16, 7). This food from heaven had often been evoked in Israel's historical and sapiential traditions, and in her

[9] Cf. A. Feuillet, *Etudes johanniques* (Bruges, 1962), pp. 72-6; R. Bultmann, *op. cit.*, pp. 164ff.

[10] G. Ziener, "Weisheitbuch und Johannesevangelium," in *Biblica* 38 (1957), pp. 396-418; 39 (1958), pp. 37-60; I de la Potterie, "L'arrière-fond du thème johannique de vérité," in *Studia évangélica* (Berlin, 1959), pp. 279-94; F. M. Braun, *Jean le Théologian* (Paris, 1964), II, pp. 115-35.

[11] Jn. 1, 14: regarding the wisdom context which to a certain extent sheds light on the elaboration of the Logos doctrine, see C. Spicq, "Le Siracide et la structure littéraire du Prologue de Jean," in *Mémorial Lagrange* (Paris, 1940), pp. 183-95; F. M. Braun, *op. cit.*, pp. 138-50, also notes the connection between the title "Logos" and the title "Son of Man" (esp. pp. 146ff.).

[12] Cf. Jn. 4, 13ff. and 32; 7, 37ff. where life is assimilated to the Spirit.

liturgical formulas: "He rained manna upon them for food and gave them heavenly bread; the bread of the mighty was eaten by men" (Ps. 77 [LXX], 24f.). And since Israel's eschatological hopes were often couched in terms provided by her exodus tradition, she came to envisage a new gift of manna.[13]

In Christ's discourse (John 6), it is a scriptural citation very close to Psalm 77 that serves as the basis for a midrashic treatment. It is Christ who brings the new manna, but this new manna far surpasses that which their fathers received in the desert. To begin with, the new manna is capable of insuring a life that death can no longer affect. The old manna was an earthly food, and those who ate it are now dead (6, 50. 58). In the new era inaugurated by Jesus, however, the believer will share the very life of God. This is the gift which God accords to men through Christ's mission (6, 27. 33. 51). By his words and actions he offers the gift of eternal life to all men, and faith enables them to accept it.

"I Am the Bread of Life"

But it goes further than that. This eternal life somehow coincides with Jesus himself, and man opens up to God's gift by believing in Jesus. The Johannine discourse is tinged with this affirmation: "I am the bread of life . . . the bread that has come down from heaven" (6, 35. 42. 48-51). The expression is thus tied up with the Son-of-Man theme; in Johannine terms, the Son of Man is the one who has come down from heaven and who is ascending there again.[14] The true bread of heaven, the bread

[13] Neh. 9, 15; Pss. 105, 40; 78, 24; Wis. 16; Baruch syr. 29, 8; Syb. 7, 148f; Pesiqta 49a; Midrash Ruth 2, 14; Philo, *Mut. nom.*, 141-44. Cf. H. Dodd, *The Interpretation of the Fourth Gospel* (Cambridge, 1953), pp. 333ff.; R. Meyer, *"Manna,"* in *TWNT* IV, pp. 466-70.

[14] R. Schnackenburg: "The Son of Man is the Johannine Messiah, the giver of life (the real bread of life of Chapter 6) and the judge who already exercises these functions now. Indeed, only he can exercise them, because he is the Son of Man who has come down from heaven and who is ascending there again": *The Gospel According to St. John* I (London and New York, 1968), p. 53. E. M. Sidebottom, *The Christ of the Fourth Gospel* (London, 1961), pp. 84ff.; Colpe, "Ho huios tou anthrōpou," in *TWNT* VIII, pp. 468-74.

which can truly offer eternal life to men, is the Son of Man himself insofar as his origin is in heaven. One must belong to the sphere of divine realities in order to be able to introduce man to it.

Consequently, the one and only condition for receiving life is faith in the Son of Man. Starting out from the sign, man must learn to recognize and put his unreserved trust in the Father's envoy.[15] But this faith does not come easily. It is not easy to recognize this man, whose human origins are known, as a divine being: "Is this not Jesus the son of Joseph, whose father and mother we know? How then does he say, 'I have come down from heaven'?" (6, 42).[16]

Faith, far from abstracting from Jesus' human reality, must recognize in him the very presence of God. John reacts against the docetist tendencies that are beginning to crop up; he underlines and stresses the reality of the incarnation of God's only Son. Faith means recognizing the Son of Man in Jesus of Nazareth; the flesh of Jesus is the sign of eternal life.

We must add that this faith is not simply a human process of development. It is achieved only by those who are brought to it by the Father, by virtue of their fidelity to truths already perceived.[17]

"My Flesh for the Life of the World"

Verses 48-51 pick up the main themes brought out so far: "I am the bread of life. Your fathers ate the manna in the desert, and have died. This is the bread that comes down from heaven, so that if anyone eat of it he will not die." But suddenly a new horizon opens up: "And indeed (*kai . . . de*), the bread that I will give is my flesh for the life of the world (*huper tēs tou kosmou zōēs*)" (6, 51c).

In the fourth gospel, the word "flesh" connotes everything that goes to make up the reality of man, with all his potentialities and weaknesses. John used this word in his prologue to express the

---

[15] R. Schnackenburg, *op. cit.*, pp. 508-24 (bibliog. p. 509).
[16] E. M. Sidebottom, *op. cit.*, pp. 97f.; 166ff.
[17] Jn. 6, 44; 7, 17; 10, 4f.; 18, 37; 3, 19-21; 8, 43f.

incarnation of the eternal Logos (1, 14). The other phrase, "for the life of the world", is tied up with a great Christian tradition; it connotes the death of Christ and its redemptive value.[18] Thus there is a tieup between the fact that Jesus is the source of eternal life for believers and the fact that he died on the cross; [19] that is why he talks about the bread that he *will give* (dōsō). The full accomplishment of his salvific activity is tied up with the glorification that comes about through his death (7, 39).

But perhaps we must go even further here. Verse 51c recalls, to a certain extent, the formula for the institution of the eucharist which was handed down in the communities of Asia and which Paul and Luke, at any rate, bore witness to: [20] "This is my body which is being given for you" (Luke 22, 19). John, to be sure, is the only one to use the word "flesh" in talking about the eucharist. But we know that the word "body" was unknown in Hebrew and Aramaic, and that the word *"bashar/bishra"* could certainly be translated into Greek as *sarx*.

Are we dealing here with an independent liturgical tradition, as Dodd and some others feel? [21] Or should we attribute to John himself the use of this formula, of which the other New Testament traditions are unaware? [22] Or should we regard it as the expression of an anti-docetist theology which spotlights the salvific import of the incarnation? [23] My own feeling is that, despite some typically Johannine retouches ("for the life of the world"),

[18] Riesenfeld, "Huper," in TWNT VIII, pp. 510ff.; H. Schürmann, "Johan. 6, 51c: ein Schlüssel zur johanneischen Brotrede," in *BZ* 2 (1958), pp. 244-62.

[19] Cf. Jn. 10, 11. 15; 11, 50ff.; 15, 13; 17, 19; 18, 14; 1 Jn. 3, 16.

[20] Cf. 1 Cor. 11, 24; J. Jeremias, *Die Abendmahlsworte Jesu* (Zurich, 1949²), pp. 67-103; P. Neuenzeit, *Das Herrenmahl* (Munich, 1960), pp. 105ff.

[21] C. H. Dodd, *Historical Tradition in the Fourth Gospel* (Cambridge, 1963), pp. 58ff.: "We may, therefore, with great probability take John 6, 51 to be derived not from any reminiscence of the synoptic passion narrative but from a liturgical tradition going back independently to the Aramaic of the Church's earliest days."

[22] The expression appears in Ignatius of Antioch: Rom. 7, 3; Sm. 7, 1; Phld. 4, 1; Trall. 8, 1. And in Justin, Apol. 1, 66.

[23] G. H. MacGregor, "The Eucharist in the Fourth Gospel," in *NTSt.* 9 (1962/3), pp. 111-19; E. Schweizer, "sōma," in *TWNT* VII, p. 138.

we have here a very clear allusion to the formula of institution.[24] Thus, although there is no account in the context of the last supper, John knew about it; and he regarded the eucharist as the memorial of the paschal event. But here the stress is not so much on the notion of oblation or sacrifice; it is on the notion of self-giving, out of love, for the life of men in this world.[25]

"The Flesh of the Son of Man"

Following a technique that is typically Johannine, the debate is sparked once again by a question from Jesus' audience. They assert that they are incapable of understanding such a proposal. In his reply Jesus underlines and stiffens his claim: "Amen, amen, I say to you, unless you eat (*fagēte*) the flesh of the Son of Man and drink his blood, you shall not have life in you. He who eats (*trōgōn*) my flesh and drinks my blood has life everlasting, and I will raise him up on the last day" (6, 54-55).

Here we again find most of the themes presented in the earlier verses, and now the whole preceding development is given a eucharistic cast. As we have already noted, it is clear that the evangelist is explicitly referering here to participation in the eucharist. He talks about eating and drinking conjointly (as early as verse 35), and the vocabulary becomes very realistic. The verb *trōgō* means "to chew, to munch". The text suggests that, in the last analysis, it is the eating of the eucharistic bread which most clearly effects our participation in the life offered to us by Jesus, the Son of Man.

There is a real continuity between the doctrine of the incarnation (i.e., of the Son of Man and Logos) and the doctrine of the eucharist. The eucharist represents the flesh insofar as it is the locus and the sign of the Son of Man who has come down from heaven to bring us back there with him. That is why the eucharist is also the source of the resurrection to come. In offering the eucharistic bread, the paschal Christ offers himself as the source

[24] O. Betz, *Die Eucharistie in der Zeit der griechischen Väter* (Freiburg im Br., 1961). II/I, pp. 181f.
[25] *Ibid.*, 178, n. 658.

of eternal life; it is he who, on the last day, will complete what he now begins in the life of men who have true faith. The eucharist can only be understood in the framework of Christology as a whole.

In the last analysis, of course, life is not an end in itself. The fourth gospel is not preaching some sort of supernatural vitalism. To live is to enter into communion with the Son and, through him, into communion with the Father. It is an exchange of mutual knowledge and mutual love that is given stability and definitiveness.[26] Eternal life is a love that nothing can ever demolish; and the eucharistic meal is the privileged moment for its first realization in time.[27]

The Flesh and the Spirit

At the end of this discourse, the opposition of many listeners is registered forcefully: "This is a hard saying. Who can listen to it?" (6, 61). They are not just reacting against his last words about eating his flesh, and Jesus does not try to rebut a charge of cannibalism. They are actually reacting against his whole teaching in the discourse. The major difficulty is acknowledging in the humanity of Jesus the presence of the Son of Man, whose being is divine. His words about his eucharistic body only push the problem to its extreme limit.

Their reproach provides the occasion for a final and most important elaboration: "Does this scandalize you? What then if you should see the Son of Man ascending where he was before? It is the Spirit that gives life; the flesh profits nothing. The words that I have spoken to you are spirit and life" (6, 63-64). We are face to face with the scandal that Jesus is, with the great decision for or against faith (6, 64-70).

The statement of Jesus remains uncompleted, but it opens up a broad horizon: "What then if you should see the Son of Man ascending where he was before?" The re-ascent of the Son of

---

[26] Cf. J. Heise, *Bleiben: Menein in den Johanneischen Schriften* (Tübingen, 1967), pp. 92f.
[27] Cf. Jn. 15, 1ff. One might also bring in Apoc. 3, 20.

Man is an integral part of John's theology. Jesus is a divine, pre-existent being, who shares in the Father's glory from the beginning (17, 5. 24). He comes down from heaven and takes on human flesh, but only to bring it into glory through the cross and allow "all flesh" to enter into communion with him (17, 1-5).

In association with the Son-of-Man theme, the verb *anabainō* expresses the entrance of the man Jesus into glory (1, 51; 3, 13ff.; 20, 17). It is in the transfiguration of Jesus' humanity that his words will take on their full meaning. The Christ who gives eternal life, the Christ we eat in the eucharist, is the Christ who has entered the glory of the resurrection through his death on the cross.[28] The eucharist is the sacrament of the risen one, the sacrament of glory.

Verse 63 spells out a further point: "It is the spirit that gives life; the flesh profits nothing." The antithesis between flesh and (divine) spirit plays a critical role in John's gospel (3, 3ff.). The glorification of Christ will bring the gift of the Spirit to believers. He will enable them to live in real communion with Christ and the Father.[29]

That is why the risen Christ, possessing the fullness of the Spirit, is able to share it ever more fully with those who open up and accept him in faith. That is also why the eucharist is the sacrament which gives the spirit and transforms the flesh. Here we have a line of thought which the theology of *epiclesis* will use to good advantage.[30]

[28] Cf. Jn. 7, 39; 15, 26; 16, 5-5; 20, 22.

[29] Jn. 20, 23; 1, 32f; 3, 34.

[30] Y. Congar, "Les deux formes du pain de vie dans l'evangile et la tradition," in *Parole de Dieu et sacerdoce* (Tournai, 1962), pp. 21-58.

Angelo Penna, C.R.L./*Rome, Italy*

Eucharist and Mass

t is with some bitterness that St. Paul observes in 1 Corinthians 14, 23 that if a pagan or anyone uninitiated were to come to a meeting where the gift of tongues were being exercised unchecked, he would think they were all mad. The same would probably be true if a modern Christian were to be present at any of the meetings described by St. Paul, irrespective of whether he understood the language or not. If, on the other hand, he were to be present at a Mass in the 4th or 5th centuries, he would be equally astonished, but for the opposite reason this time. In Rome, Milan and in virtually the whole of the Latin world, Christians recited prayers, read pieces of Scripture, sung psalms and performed gestures which are practically the same as were used until only a few years ago, when modern languages were introduced. The history of the liturgy may give the impression that there was a complex relationship which linked the various local traditions, and that the various formulae and gestures were only slowly introduced; and the temptation is to conclude that there was no single guiding line of development, but rather it was spasmodic and inconsistent. However, the changes actually were few, limited more or less exclusively to the variable parts, whose variations were necessary to give as wide a range of teaching as possible in the readings and to provide a sufficient choice of prayers and chants acceptable to the many assemblies, with their different cultures and traditions.

The canon also, especially if understood in the wider sense (from the preface to the communion), has its own history. But to all intents and purposes it was already complete in its essentials for the Latin Church by the time of Gregory the Great. Gregory, who introduced the *Our Father,* also passed on to us a much debated detail concerning the origin of the canon, which he attributed to an unknown scholasticus,[1] i.e., an educated person or some private individual. There is little further information, since he does not give the date of composition nor the reason for its adoption by the Church; it is also a very surprising piece of information, since we have evidence [2] of the belief that the canon went back to the apostles themselves—note, for example, the titles *"Apostolic* Constitutions" and *"Apostolic* Tradition".

Mass in the 4th Century

Even without the references in the Fathers, it is still possible to have a reasonable idea of the shape of the Mass at this time from some of the classic works, such as (for the Eastern Church) the *Eucology of Serapion,* the *Catecheses* of Cyril of Jerusalem and Theodore of Mopsuestia, and the *Apostolic Constitutions,* and (for the West) St. Ambrose's *De Sacramentis* and *De Mysteriis.*

The *De Sacramentis* is a treatise, mostly theological in approach, on baptism, the eucharist and prayer, and it describes the rite of consecration, mentioning also the prayers which immediately precede and follow the consecration. In a form which differs only slightly from our contemporary wording, St. Ambrose [3] quotes after the preface the prayer *Fac nobis hanc obla-*

---

[1] Epist. IX, 12; *P.L.* 77, 956ff. In the East the usage is attested by Cyril of Jerusalem, Cat. Myst. V, 11, in G. Rauschen, *Florilegium Patristicum VII, Monumenta eucharistica et liturgica vetustissima* (Bonn, 2nd ed. 1914), 70 (a further edition was published by Quasten in 1935).

[2] Cf. Vigilius Epist. ad Eutherium 5, *P.L.* 69, 18.

[3] De Sacramentis, IV, 5-6, in Rauschen, *op. cit.,* 124ff. On the prayers and gestures (from the kiss of peace at the anaphora to the memento of the dead and the prayer of the faithful) cf. A. Piedagnel, *Cyrille de Jérusalem, Catéchèses Mystagogiques* (*Sources Chrétiennes* 126), Paris,

tionem (= *Quam Oblationem*), the memorial of the last supper, the *Qui Pridie,* and the repetition of the words and gestures of Christ at that meal, and the *Ergo Memores* (=*Unde et Memores*). There are missing the prayers for the living and the dead and the beginning of the canon, but witness to these can be found elsewhere, and silence certainly cannot be held to argue their non-existence.

The same content is to be found more or less in the *De Mysteriis.* The author uses types from the Old Testament and makes comparisons with other miracles to prove that the words of Christ effect what they signify, i.e., they change the bread and wine into the body and blood of Christ, because "the power of the blessing is greater than the power of nature". Ambrose mentions [4] the psalms usually sung or at least recited at the beginning of each celebration and he quotes some verses of Psalms 42 and 22. Such would appear to be the general outline of the introductory part with its chants, which no doubt were interspersed between readings from the Old and New Testaments, before the homily of the "president" (cf. Justin, Apol. I, 67, 3ff).

The rite of communion for the Eastern Church is described in the *Apostolic Constitutions,* VIII, 13, 11-15, 10. The bishop gives the warning: "The holy things are for the holy," and the people reply with acclamations in praise of the one Holy One, and the one Lord, Jesus Christ, and they say the opening words of the *Gloria,* the *Hosanna,* etc. Communion is distributed in a fixed order: bishop, presbyters, deacons, subdeacons, lectors, cantors, ascetics, deaconesses, virgins, widows, youth, and the whole people. The bishop offers the bread, saying: "The body of Christ," and the recipient says: "Amen." The deacon offers the chalice, saying: "The blood of Christ, chalice of life," and the

---

1966, 150-9, where use is also made of the testimony of St. John Chrysostom and Theodore of Mopsuestia. On the development of such formulas cf. L. Ligier, "Dalla Cena di Gesù all'anafora della Chiesa," in *Riv. Liturgica* 53 (1966), pp. 480-521; P. Borella, "Evoluzione letteraria del Canone romano," *ibid.,* pp. 522-58.

[4] De myst., 9, 50; 8, 43; cf. Cyril, Cat. Myst., V, 1-18 in Rauschen, *op. cit.* 94. 92. 64-75.

reply again is "Amen." Psalm 33 is sung, and there follows the thanksgiving.

The whole ceremony is presupposed by St. Cyril,[5] who emphasizes the faith needed to recognize the symbol (*antitypos*) of the body and blood of Christ, and also the necessity of an attitude of reverence. He insists on the position of the hands and the care necessary to avoid any crumb or drop of wine falling, and he also refers to the thanksgiving.[6] On the externals of the celebration, much detailed information can be found in the *Didascalia Apostolorum* (II, 57, 2-11), while the older texts, the *Apologia* of Justin and the *Didaché,* are less explicit, although they do contain prayer formulas and refer to the sacred nature of the rite.

Hippolytus' *Apostolic Tradition* gives us much important information. The consecration, called *oblatio* in the Latin text and *prosphora* in the Eastern texts,[7] is accompanied by prayers which may be looked upon as foreshadowing the future Roman canon. A description of communion is given both in the section on baptism and also in the section on the Sunday liturgy.[8] There is a third reference to it, when the author mentions the common meal or agape, saying that "it is a question of an *eulogia,* not of the eucharist, symbol of the body of the Lord".[9] Toward the end of the work, Hippolytus lays down that communion should be re-

[5] Cat. Myst. V, 19-22, in Rauschen, *op. cit.* 75-8. Theodore of Mopsuestia describes and comments on the position of the hands, cf. Tonneau-Devreesse, *Les Homélies Catéchétiques de Théodore de Mopsueste,* (*Studi e Testi* 145), Città del Vaticano, 1949, 577.

[6] This thanksgiving could have been directed by the charistics, cf. *Didaché* 10, 7; Justin, Apol. I, 67, 5 in Rauschen, *op. cit.* 14, 18; also in later times considerable liberty was allowed over the composition of the formulary, cf. B. Botte, *La Tradition Apostolique de Saint Hippolyte* (Münster im W., 1963), 28, 30. For the care needed to prevent any crumbs or drops of wine falling cf. Tertull., De Corona, 3, 4; Jerome, Tract. de Ps. 147, in *Corp. Christ.* 2, 1043; 78, 338.

[7] Cf. B. Botte, *op. cit.* 10-17; J. A. Jungmann, *Liturgie der christlichen Frühzeit* (Freiburg im Sch., 1967), 78.

[8] Cf. B. Botte, *op. cit.,* 60; *Didaché* 14, 1; Justin, Apol. I, 67, 7, Rauschen, *op. cit.,* 14, 19. After baptism a small quantity of milk and honey was given to the new Christian, cf. B. Botte, *op. cit.,* 56-8, the epitaph of Pectorius in Rauschen, *op. cit.,* 22, and Tertull., Dec Corona, 3. 3, in *Corp. Christ.* 2, 1042.

[9] B. Botte, *op. cit.,* 66, 82-5.

ceived fasting and with the greatest care, in case any drops should fall and be profaned; and just before this, referring to the custom of sending or taking home the consecrated bread, he urges that any danger of profanation by an unbeliever or animal be avoided. Here then we have a witness to the keeping of the eucharist and communion outside mass.

Eucharistia and Eulogia

In the Old Testament, the word *eucharisteîn* (and *eucharistia*) includes not only the idea of thanksgiving but also the idea of praising God and extolling his creative activity and his actions on behalf of the Jews. In practice it is synonymous with *eulogeîn* (to praise or bless) and its corresponding noun, thus justifying Audet's conclusion [10] that the literary genre of the "eucharistic" prayer of the *Didaché* is the same as the Jewish "Blessing", understood as praise of God and worship of the action of God.

The two words frequently occur in the writings of the Fathers. Both often contain the idea of thanskgiving or praise, but only in *eulogia* does the idea of blessing predominate. And then both may refer to the consecration or to the eucharistic elements, both before and after the narrative of the last supper.[11] The use of *eulogia* as applying directly to the sacrament can be found in Origen, Cyril of Jerusalem, and in various liturgical texts and in some apocrypha (especially the *Acts of St. Thomas the Apostle*). But the two words gradually ceased to be interchangeable, as is implicit in the use made of them by Hippolytus, who employs them as opposites. He lays down [12] the following norms for the *eulogia:* the bishop is to preside; there are to be prayers and

---

[10] *La Didaché, Instructions des Apôtres* (Paris, 1958) 375-97; idem, *Genre littéraire et formes cultuelles de l'Eucharistie*, "Nova et Vetera", in *Eph. Lit.*, 80 (1966), 352-85.

[11] For the meaning of *eulogia* cf. G. W. Lampe, *A Patristic Lexicon*, fasc. 2 (Oxford, 1962), 569ff; for the use of *eucharistia* with this meaning cf. *Didaché*, 9, 1; Ignatius, Ad Smyrnaeos, 7, 1; Justin, Apol., I, 66, 1; Iren., Adv. Haer., IV, 18, 5, in G. Rauschen, *op. cit.*, 11; 16. 169. 172.

[12] B. Botte, *op. cit.*, 64-8.

chants, and blessed bread is to be distributed to the faithful. Referring to the evening meal in common, after describing the arrangement of the *eulogia,* Hippolytus says that the rite cannot be performed by lay people. The context shows that in the *Apostolic Tradition,* the *eulogia* has taken the place of the primitive agape, or the "ordinary, innocent" meal mentioned by Pliny (Epist. X, 96, 7).[13]

The eucharist and *eulogia* had a deep social, ecclesial meaning. Those present received, as a body, at least the *eulogia.*[14] Moreover (cf. Justin, Apol. I, 67, 5), the eucharist was taken by the deacons to the Christians who were not present at the liturgical assembly. Later the custom seems to have become restricted. The consecrated bread sent in this way was meant to symbolize esteem and identity of faith. Identity of faith, it should be noted, referred to the essentials of belief, not to possible differences concerning various practices (cf. the reference by Irenaeus[15] to the sending of the eucharist by Victor's predecessors to some supporters of the Quartodecimans). Later the custom of the *fermentum* spread; the *Liber Pontificalis*[16] attributes it to Miltiades and Siricius. Siricius is claimed to have forbidden any celebration without the adding of the particle consecrated by the bishop (*fermentum*). Under Innocent I,[17] a different custom made its appearance in Rome: only the presbyters in the city received the *fermentum,* and not those who were out in the *paroeciae* or cemetery churches, thus avoiding too long a journey with the *sacramenta.*

A significant development in the *eulogia* took place when the custom was introduced of sending a part of the simple common

[13] *Ibid.,* 72.
[14] Augustine (*De peccatorum meritis et remissione* II, 42, in *C.S.C.L.,* 60, 113) points out that it is right to give blessed bread to catechumens, even if it is not a sacrament in the modern sense, since it is nevertheless more holy than any other food.
[15] Cf. Eusebius, *Hist. Eccl.,* V. 24, 15; *P.G.,* 20, 505.
[16] Ed. L. Duchesne, I, Paris, 1886 (reprinted 1955), 168, 216; on the similar usage to be found in the Eastern church, cf. E. Peterson, "Meris. Hostien Partikel und Opfer-Anteil," in *Eph. Lit.,* 61 (1947), 3-12.
[17] Epist. 25 ad Dec., 5, 6; *P.L.* 20, 556ff.

meal to those who had not been present.[18] According to the *Apostolic Constitutions* (VIII, 31, 2), it is to be seen as something more than a symbol of moral unity, since it had a clear social and charitable purpose. However, the symbolic meaning remained and indeed often predominated, as can be seen from the *eulogia* used by the monks and from the norms put forward by Hincmar in the 9th century.[19] The term *eulogia*, often used in connection with devotion to particular martyrs or sanctuaries, was also used to refer to a private devotional practice. Some personage, usually a bishop, blessed a loaf and sent it to a friend as a sign of intimate, spiritual union, and this, as distinct from the eucharist,[20] became *eulogia* once received in the appropriate manner.[21]

The Supper of the Lord

This expression is Pauline in origin (1 Cor. 11, 20ff.); comparing this meal with an ordinary meal serves to show its own peculiar characteristics. The dramatic side of the last supper is recalled in considerable detail and this leaves no room for doubting that the rite is essentially an anamnesis or commemoration (cf. Lk. 22, 18; 1 Cor. 11, 24). The escape from Egypt (which still retained its function as a type) is replaced by the redemption of the human race. This idea now lies at the heart of the pasch (1 Cor. 5, 7). With or without the reference to the Servant of Yahweh, the identification of Christ with the paschal lamb is a common theme (cf. Jn. 1, 29. 36; 19, 36; Acts 8, 32; 1 Pet. 1, 19), and is basic to the Apocalypse with its twofold image of the lamb that is sacrificed and the lamb in glory.

The eucharist appears from the very beginning as connected with this Christology. The celebration of the eucharist is characterized primarily by the idea of the "blessing" or hymn recalling

[18] Cf. M. Righetti, *Storia liturgica,* III (Milan, 2nd ed. 1956), 473-6.
[19] Capitulum 7; *P.L.* 125, 774.
[20] Cf. Paulinus of Nola, Ep., 5, 21 in *C.S.C.L.* 29, 38ff.
[21] Cf. *idem,* Ep., 3, 6; 4, 5, in *C.S.C.L.,* 18, 24; Augustine, Ep. 31, 9, in *C.S.C.L.,* 34, 2, 8.

the wonders worked by God, and it is the means of thanking or blessing God for the achievement of the new David, the Servant of Yahweh, who has revealed the divine plan of salvation (*Didaché*, 9, 2; 10, 2). The memorial reaches its peak in the retelling of the death of the redeemer (1 Cor. 11, 25), viewed both theologically and as an historic event, and as the seal of the new covenant (cf. Jer. 31, 31ff). The ecclesial implications of all this gradually became clearer: a new relationship between God and man was now established, as man becomes a sharer in the kingdom of heaven. In the Roman canon, similar ideas are expressed in the prayers which precede (the *Qui Pridie*) and follow (the Ergo Memores = *Unde et Memores*) the consecration. The whole formula, in spite of subsequent development and retouching, can be traced back to the *Apostolic Tradition*.[22]

Sacrifice of the New Covenant

The idea eucharist=sacrifice (cf. 1 Cor. 10, 16-21) is often expressed in fairly technical terms.[23] The epiclesis in the *Apostolic Constitutions* (VIII, 12, 39) prays that God will graciously accept the offered gifts and send the Holy Spirit on the sacrifice which is about to be performed. In the early texts, the idea of sacrifice predominates (*De Sac.* IV, 5, 21; V, 1, 1). Besides praying that the offering be received, the text also underlines the difference between the eucharistic sacrifice and the type offered by Melchisedech. Cyril[24] speaks of a *spiritual sacrifice* and of an *unbloody worship for our sins*. In the *Eucology of Serapion* (II, 11) it is called a *living sacrifice*, an *unbloody offering*. The term sacrifice can be found as early as the *Didaché* (14, 1, 3), which also says explicitly that the rite fulfills the prophecy of Malachy (1, 11) about *the clean sacrifice*. Hippolytus,[25] who insists on

---

[22] B. Botte, *op. cit.*, 14ff.

[23] It does not follow that the word *eucharistia* of itself indicates a sacrifice; the discussion revolves around a text of Phil, *De specialibus legibus* I, 224, edited by L. Cohn, V, 55 where mention is made of hymns, praise and other *eucharistiae*.

[24] Cat. Myst., V, 8, 10 in Rauschen, *op. cit.* 68, 70.

[25] B. Botte, *op. cit.*, 10, 54.

the idea of thanksgiving, mentions the sacrificial "offering" three times. Justin, like the *Didaché*, quotes [26] the text from Malachy, and albeit briefly develops the typology of the bloodless sacrifices of the Old Law and the eucharist. St. Irenaeus follows a similar line and, like later writers, sees the offering of the bread and wine as a true sacrifice, much more perfect and acceptable to God than the sacrifices in blood of the Old Testament.[27]

This inclusion of the rite among truly sacrificial acts explains why some writers insist so much on the connection between personal offering and sharing in communion. This, too, is the origin of the custom of a procession of communicants bringing forward the offerings.[28] In the earliest texts, these offerings are linked rather with the agape or its prolongation in the shape of food collected in the church and sent to the poor. But undoubtedly there was also a direct link with communion. The mode of communion and the large numbers of faithful made a certain abundance of bread inevitable. For this reason St. Cyril [29] and St. Caesarius [30] attack those wealthy people who excuse themselves from not presenting any "sacrifice", and then steal part of the offerings of those less fortunately situated than themselves.

The Symbolic Meanings Seen in the Rite

From early days the prayers of the canon have emphasized the commemorative nature of the rite, with some emphasis also on its figurative or eschatological nature, already present in St. Paul (1 Cor. 11, 26). The *Apostolic Constitutions* (VIII, 12, 38) combines both aspects: "Recalling, therefore, his passion and death, his resurrection from the dead and return to heaven, and his future second coming, in which he will come in glory and power to judge the living and the dead and to render to each according to his works (Rom. 2, 6), we offer to thee, king and God, etc." The purpose is to draw attention, above all, to the

---

[26] Dial. cum Tryphone, 41, in Rauschen, *op. cit.*, 169ff.
[27] Adv. Haer., V. 17, 5, in Rauschen, *op. cit.*, 171.
[28] Cf. N. and R. Boulet, *Eucharistie ou Messe* (Paris, 1953), 202.
[29] De Op. et Elym., 15, *C.S.C.L.*, 3, 1, 384.
[30] Sermo 13, 2, in *Corp. Christ.* 103, 65.

effects of the suffering and death of Christ; this is the same theology of the redemption as is to be found in the *De Sacramentis*
(IV, 6, 28), "If we proclaim his death, we proclaim the remission of sins. If every time blood is sprinkled, it is done for the
remission of sins, I ought always to receive this blood for the
remission of my sins. Since I always sin, I ought always to take
the medicine." This explicit mention of the remission of sins and
the expiatory value of the passion of Christ may be taken as a
comment on the words of St. John, "I am the living bread which
has come down from heaven. Anyone who eats this bread will
live forever, and the bread that I shall give is my flesh for the life
of the world."

The most primitive texts (cf. Rom. 12, 5; 1 Cor. 12, 12-23)
are at pains to show how the union of the faithful, considered as
one body, is symbolized in the bread and cup of wine, which are
made up of a great number of smaller grains or drops.[31] In the
liturgy, the accent was rather on the idea of an eschatological
union of believers, even resorting to the idea of the diaspora, the
parallel being based on the diverse origin of the component
parts. The *Eucology of Serapion* adopts this idea from the
Didaché (9, 4) in the prayer for the "one, living Catholic
Church"; and at the same time it expresses concern that there
should be belief in the same doctrine and peace in the community.

The eucharist is a symbol of unity for St. Ignatius also, though
in a different sense. Concerned over the more or less heretical
divisions among believers, he urges (Ad Philadelphenses, 4) the
celebration of only one *eucharistia,* and reminds them that *the
flesh* of Christ is one, *the chalice* is one, as *the altar* and *bishop* are
one also. So many symbols of unity suppose the greatest efforts
to maintain harmony. The term *eucharist* was taken by Ignatius
to refer to the whole assembly of Christians, during which the
bread and wine were consecrated. The appeal for unity (*Strive
to have only one eucharist*) may have had a practical, moral
purpose; a little before there is an allusion (cc. 2-3) to division
and "schisms". According to Ignatius, the one eucharist presup-

[31] Cf. Aug., Sermo 227, *P.L.,* 38, 1100.

posed a precise hierarchy, which was to be respected. The con-celebration had as president the bishop, and the whole com-munity was united around its own clergy. Such a union, under the bishop as president, was required by Ignatius for the agape (cf. Ad Smyrnaeos 8, 2). Continuous discord was taken as being a rejection of the eucharist, and as a kind of death, to be rem-edied by a return to genuine charity (cf. Ad Smyrnaeos 7, lff.). And it is precisely the eucharist which Ignatius describes as being the source of "incorruptible charity" (Ad Romanos, 7. 3).

The Eucharist Merely a Symbol?

The question arises whether such abundant symbolism is a possible indication that the body and blood of Christ were be-lieved to be present in a merely symbolic manner. In the early writers there are turns of phrase which would seem to indicate an answer in the affirmative. They view the consecrated elements as a "figure" of some truth or reality. The Greek authors use the terms *homoioma*,[32] *antitypos*,[33] *symbolon*,[34] while the Latin au-thors use *similitudo* or *figura*.[35] However, that such a vocabu-lary was not really compatible with belief in the real presence would seem to be indicated by the fact that it became ever more rare until eventually it dropped out of use altogether. Some au-thors are clear enough: their use of such symbolism in no way implies a denial of the reality of the real presence. Cyril of Jeru-salem, among others, is quite unequivocal, since a few lines previously he compares the miracle of the eucharist with Cana, precisely to show the reality of the presence of Christ's body and blood. And indeed realism can be shown to exist even in writers

[32] Cf. B. Botte, *op. cit.*, 34ff.; *Eucology of Serapion* III, 12, in Rauschen, *op. cit.* 29ff.

[33] Cyr. Jerus., Cat. Myst., V. 20, in Rauschen, *op. cit.*, 76.

[34] Cf. Cyr. Jerus. Cat. Myst. V. 20 in Rauschen *op. cit.*, 59 (and also 29, note 2), and Origen, In Matt., XI, 14, *P.G.* 13, 952, who speaks of the body as being "a type and symbol".

[35] Cf. De Sac. IV, 5, 21; Tertull. Adv. Marcionem, IV, 40, 3, in Rauschen, *op. cit.*, 124, 180; cf also the variant versions of the prayer *Quam Oblationem* in P. Batiffol, *Etudes d'histoire et de théologie positive, II, L'Eucharistie. La présence réelle et la transubstantiation* (Paris 9e, 1930), 361-63.

who favor allegoric interpretations, such as Clement of Alexandra and Origen.[36] The biggest difficulty is in interpreting Tertullian,[37] but it does not seem that he in fact denied the concrete reality of the real presence; his purpose was only to point out that the bread, considered as a visible thing, was a symbol of Christ's body. It is also difficult to decide exactly how far such writers, especially the Alexandrine Fathers, were influenced by the platonic theory of real things as *paradeigmata* or *homoiomata* (models or likenesses) of the ideas (Plato, Parmenides 132d).

Generally speaking, it is Justin's ideas which underlie the prayers of the liturgy, from the *Apostolic Tradition* to the *Apostolic Constitutions* and the various canons; he emphasizes the difference between the eucharistic bread and ordinary bread and he views the eucharist as the body of Christ and food of the soul. Origen [38] speaks of "eucharistized" bread, i.e., bread which has been transformed by the prayer into a "body which is holy, and makes men holy". The *Eucology of Serapion* (III, 13) is able to call the eucharist *"homoioma* of the death" of Christ, inasmuch as it is a commemorative sign; but it does not therefore cease to be a real *bloodless sacrifice* and the *body of the Word,* phrases which occur in the same anaphora along with the expressions: *medicine of life, medicine for every sickness,* thus echoing the definition of St. Ignatius (Ad Ephesios, 20, 2), "Medicine of immortality, medicine given that we may not die but rather live forever in Jesus Christ."

[36] Cf. P. Batiffol, *op. cit.,* 248-84.
[37] For the lofty concept Tertullian had of the eucharist cf. De. Idololatria, 7, 1-3; De Corona, 3, 4, in *Corp. Christ.* 2, 1106, 1043.
[38] Contra Celsum VIII, 33; *P.G.* 11, 1565.

Victor Warnach, O.S.B./*Maria Laach, Austria*

Symbol and Reality in the Eucharist

The reality of the presence in the eucharist has become a subject of special concern, not to say of conflict, in modern theology. Both symbolic and realist interpretations confront one another even within the same confession. The background and motives for these differences are extremely diverse, but for the most part they stem from differences in the history of ideas and ways of understanding the world. While the deeper study of these factors cannot be the object of this article, some reference to them cannot be avoided if we are to appreciate the different positions. Our principal aim, however, is to rethink traditional teaching in the light of the bible.

1. *Biblical Evidence*

The many different ways of referring to the eucharistic mystery in the New Testament have been portrayed in the preceding articles in this volume of *Concilium*. They show that these refer primarily to an *action* of the community which has come together for a meal to commemorate the Lord; thus we have the "breaking of bread" (Acts 2, 42. 46; 20, 7. 11; 27, 35; 1 Cor. 10, 16) or the Lord's supper (1 Cor. 11, 20).[1] Even expressions such as

[1] The word *eucharistia* is not used in the New Testament with the concrete meaning to be found in later theology, starting with Ignatius and Justin (*Eph.* 13, 1; *Phld.* 4; *Smyrn.* 7, 1; 8, 1; Justin *Apol.*, I, 65. 67),

"the Lord's table" (1 Cor. 10, 21) or the "chalice of the Lord" (*loc. cit.*) and the "chalice of blessing" (the blessing-cup, 1 Cor. 10, 16) are to be understood not in a static but in a dynamic sense, for, as their context proves, they refer to the cultic sacrificial meal as does the "gift from heaven" (Heb. 6, 4) and the "food from the altar (Heb. 13, 10).²

The references to the eucharist in the Old Testament are also diverse and for the most part typological. Many Fathers and theologians and not least the liturgists (see the Roman canon prayer *Supra quae*) saw in Abel's sacrifice of the first fruits of the fields, acceptable to God because of the purity of his offering, the earliest type of the eucharistic food offering in which the most pure sacrificial body of the incarnate Son of God was signified, present and offered in a manner that fulfilled this sign. Since Cyprian's time the sacrifice of bread and wine offered by Melchizedek, "the priest of the Most High God", was singled out as a prototype of the eucharist. The manna of the desert wandering only really became the "bread from heaven" and the "bread of angels" in the eucharist (Jn. 6, 31f; Ps. 78 [77], 25). Similarly, the water from the rock that Moses struck only became the "spiritual water" from the rock which is Christ (1 Cor. 10, 4). The offering of the substitute ram in the place of Isaac was paralleled with the substitution of Christ for mankind, fallen and subject to death through sin in their understanding of the symbolism of the eucharistic sacrificial mystery. Christ is both the Lamb of God who bears away the sins of the world and the

---

apart from an improbable reading of the text of 1 Cor. 10, 16 (and perhaps 1 Cor. 14, 16) where it could refer to the principal liturgical prayer. Generally, in the New Testament it means "thanksgiving" in general, or a "prayer of thanks" (2 Cor. 9, 12, etc.) where a reference to the Lord's supper could well be included. Since it is only once used to mean "thankfulness" (Acts 24, 3) it clearly carries dynamic overtones. See J. A. Jungmann's article "Eucharistia" in *LThK*, III (1959²), cols. 1141f.

² If, according to recent exegesis, the last text refers principally to the saving event at Golgotha (= "altar") this need not exclude a reference to the eucharist also; see O. Kuss (*ad loc.*, 1966 p. 219), and many non-Catholic exegetes, for example, W. Manson (1951), J. Héring (1954), T. H. Robinson (1964) and O. Michel (1966) in their commentaries on this text.

ram described in Revelation (esp. 5, 6; 13, 11); he is also the Servant of God who "bore the sins of many" (Is. 53, 12) and presented himself as a guilt offering through his vicarious sufferings (Is. 53. 10).

Just as the covenant on Sinai was sealed with a great covenant sacrifice and a sacrificial meal on the holy mountain where Moses and his companions had seen God (Exod. 24, 4-11) so in the same way the permanent and eternal covenant was concluded in the blood of Christ, blood which is "the blood of the covenant" (Mk. 14, 24) shed on the cross "for many" and celebrated at the last supper. This "new covenant" is more than a mutual agreement to abide by certain obligations; it is a legacy (*testamentum*) which is at the origin and is the source of power in a new divine dispensation for a community whose law is "rooted in its heart" (cf. Jer. 31, 31-33). The paschal celebration, being both meal and sacrifice at once, foreshadows the eucharist with particular clarity. The realism involved in this Old Testament commemoration is clearer for us today than ever before,[3] but its realization in the eucharist looks to the future and is necessarily in a very primitive state. For while the freedom brought by the exodus from Egypt was experienced as a present reality, in the cultic memorial service we have to share in an exodus of Christ "from the world to the Father" (Jn. 13, 1), from this age to one to come—that is, into the true divine reality—through the eucharistic paschal event.

While it is true that the Old Testament types are founded in saving history, yet as saving deeds they are still only "*sacramenta futuri*" (J. Daniélou) foreshadowing and promising a future saving reality. They bear an eschatological character fulfilled in a proleptic fashion only in the new saving order. The eucharist is therefore the "new pure food offering" (Mal. 1, 11) which is to be offered everywhere in the name of God; it is the antitype and so the fulfillment of this prototype, but a fulfillment which points beyond itself, in the first place to the true and complete Pasch of

[3] See, for instance, P. A. H. de Boer *Gedenken und Gedächtnis in der Welt des Alten Testaments* (Stuttgart, 1962); W. Schottroff *"Gedenken" im Alten Orient und im Alten Testament* (Neukirchen, 1964).

Christ and then on to the ultimate fulfillment in the parousia of the Kyrios.

The New Testament, too, speaks figuratively of the eucharist —for instance, in the parable of the "bread of life" (Jn. 6, 26-51a) or in the symbolic actions of the multiplication of the loaves or the miracle at Cana. But the realism of the New Testament understanding of the eucharist is unmistakable, especially in some passages in Paul (e.g. 1 Cor. 11, 27-29) or in John (6, 51b-58) which have already received sufficient study in this volume.

This combination of symbolic and typological with a realistic approach to the eucharist raises the question of the relationship between the two. Does the one either exclude or minimize the other? Are they irreconcilable or is there some internal relationship between them allowing of a synthesis? To answer these questions we need to clarify our terms and especially that of "symbol" or "sign", since much misunderstanding about this problem seems to come from terminological confusion.[4]

2. Symbol and Reality

The modern usage of the word "symbol" and its derivatives is very confusing. It is frequently used to mean a pure sign (whether a semantic sign, or a logical or scientific expression, figure or term), for something which is not immediately present. The function of a sign, however, is to bring to mind the reality for which it stands. This reality is something essentially different from the sign itself. Signs are abstract and in the logic of intention, for instance, they stand at the greatest possible distance from reality. The word "symbol" is also used of the images by which we refer to supersensual realities. If we then go on to use "symbol" of "emblems" such as flags, coats of arms, insignia, and so on, this is because these, too, represent an institution, office or

[4] This idea of "reality" ought also to be investigated more closely. Since this is not practicable here the reader is referred to a forthcoming investigation (*Das Wirchlichkeitsverständnis der Gegenwart*, Salzburg, 1969) where the modern understanding of reality and the biblical terminology are both considered.

group which has some sort of power or influence. In depth-psychology "symbol" is used of suppressed elements of conscious life, or of the sublimated forms by which drives manifest themselves in dreams, neurotic traits and awkward behavior. "Symbol" here involves a greater degree of reality than the earlier examples and borders of its full significance as seen in religious and artistic traditions. Here, especially in the older cultures, it does not mean an abstract instrument of our understanding but principally a means by which a higher, frequently divine, reality is made present or accessible—a means therefore by which living contact with the "other" world can be achieved. Symbol properly so called, therefore, is not something man has chanced upon, nor the result of human invention as are most signs, but owes its symbolic character either to the created or natural order (natural symbol) or to God's presence in saving history.[5] The two worlds of God and man, heaven and earth, spirit and matter meet preeminently in the religious symbol. Even the etymology of *symbolon,* from *symballein* (to cast together), suggests this.

The "real symbol", the full correct meaning of "symbol", is therefore a form that can be experienced by the senses and through which a higher transcendent reality announces itself as present and active.[6] It is distinguishable from a sign in that it is of its nature a self-expression in which something of the reality of what is expressed, or expresses itself, is present or "appears". For this reason it is distinguishable from the mere expression through

[5] In this we differ from S. Wisse who in his learned study *Das religiöse Symbol* (Essen, 1963) describes symbol as "the sensible form by which one expresses one's experience of the transcendent holiness of God" (p. 48). We would agree that in a real symbol both the expressive and the sign function are at work, but we would insist that it is not subjective experience but an objective determination and institution that gives a symbol its character, thus uniting the symbol with that which is symbolized on an ontological level. Wisse has logically to refuse to accept this (pp. 159-73) and consequently considers the sacraments to be "exceptions" (p. 172; cf. pp. 47; 207f.).

[6] On this we agree with K. Rahner (*The Theology of the Symbol,* in *Theological Investigations IV* (1966) pp. 227-52) although Rahner's conception of symbol is wider than ours as it includes all reality: "Being is of itself necessarily symbolic since it must 'express' itself in order fully to find its own nature" (p. 224).

which some inner experience spontaneously becomes visible but whose nature can only be gathered from its effects. To be sure, as an exact phenomenological analysis shows, both the significative and the expressive function are included within the complex phenomenon of the symbol. Nevertheless its fundamental character derives from its roots in space and time; it must be the visible and sensible "appearance" (*epiphaneia*)—as an ontological presence—of a (higher) being. The use of "appearance" here neither weakens nor questions the reality of the symbolic presence—a conclusion too frequently found in platonic thinkers. Rather it emphasizes the inadequacy of the material level of being by indicating that spiritual (pneumatic) being cannot be directly present in space and time since its nature is essentially beyond the bounds of space and time. A symbol, accordingly, is the making visible and present of a reality, of its nature divisible, in a form that though inadequate, discloses what it signifies.

Our conception of what a symbol is, therefore, determines whether we see a contradiction between symbol and reality, or can conceive of the possibility of a synthesis encompassing and complementing both aspects. This latter possibility is easier to visualize if we avoid a static limitation of our concepts of "real" and "symbol"; for in worship especially the symbols are often symbolic actions, or even symbolic or mystery dramas in which the "primal deeds" or saving events can begin to realize themselves in the present.

In any case the Bible has a realistic conception of symbol; it recognizes the fact of the pure real symbol, and this not just as a meaningless survival from a heathen cult, but as a God-given means for communicating with him. The uniqueness of the means can be appreciated from the fact that the term *symbolon* is used only twice in the Greek Bible and on both occasions in a derogatory sense (Hos. 4, 12; Wis. 2, 9). Yet the Bible contains clear references to the symbolical and to the fact of the symbolical function.

We must now direct attention to an important associated word, that of *mysterion*. For Paul this means principally, though not exclusively, God's dealings with man in history through perceptible forms. Not infrequently these take on the character of symbols properly so called. The difference between *mysterion* and symbol is that the former refers principally to that which appears, that is, to the divine acts, while the latter refers to the medium in which this appearance takes place. Connected with this biblical conception of a reality which appears, inadequately, in the present is its teaching on the two aeons; it must be emphasized, however, that the future aeon, especially in Paul and John, does not succeed or run parallel to this one; the biblical viewpoint sees both as intermingled. Despite their diverse existential characters it is possible to pass from this aeon to the next "in faith" or in "the Spirit"—and the symbol often mediates this passage.

The symbol's reality necessarily excludes the metaphor, image, allegory or parable; though the type has some relationship to the symbol in that it anticipates the promised future reality in faith, and so makes it present even if only in "shadow" form (Col. 2, 17). Hebrews 10, 1 emphasizes the contrast with the *eikon* of things. "Image" here is used in the sense given it by the ancients. For them, a picture is a copy of some primal form which shows itself and mediates its form through the image, which therefore re-presents its very reality—it is not the modern "reproduction" of something else. One can understand in this context the commandment against making images. By representing God in an image man achieved power over him (Exod. 20, 4, 22f.) and consequently must be condemned as impious. But man is himself created an "image" of God (*sēlēm*) (Gen. 1, 26f; 5, 1; 9, 6) and is to represent God and his dominion of this world. The true image of God is the God-Man Christ (2 Cor. 4, 4; Col. 1, 15) since he is the very "expression (*charakter*) of his nature" (Heb. 1, 3) as the Son (*logos*). Consequently we see the Father in Christ (Jn. 14, 9) and achieve the perfection of our own image-nature through him (Rom. 8, 29; 2 Cor. 3, 18; Col. 3, 10).

The reality of the image is related (Rom. 1, 23) to the cultic realm where the *homoioma* clearly refers to the images of idols which are made after the form (*eikones*) of mortal men and beasts. The cultic significance of *homoioma* in Romans 6, 5 is very revealing. Here baptism is a cult symbol representing the death of Christ with whom we are so closely knit that we are crucified together with him (6, 6; cf. Col. 2, 12f.). If we are really to die together with Christ in baptism then his death on the cross must also be really present in the sacrament, for one cannot die with a risen Lord now glorified in heaven and who will "die no more" (Rom. 6, 9).[7] It is therefore quite possible on the basis of

[7] On this point see our essays: "Taufe und Christusgeschehen nach Römer 6" in *Archiv f. Liturgiewiss.*, 3/2 [1954] pp. 284-366, esp. pp. 302-11; and *"Die Tauflehre des Römerbriefs in der neueren theologischen Diskussion,"* ibid., 5/2 (1958) pp. 274-332, esp. pp. 297ff.; 317-23. J. Schneider in ThWbNT V (1954), cols. 191-5 has come to essentially the same conclusion after analyzing carefully the usage of *homoioma*. It often happens that when we emphasize that in baptism (as also in the eucharist) we encounter the Savior dying on the cross so that we may share in his Pasch, it is objected that this is impossible since the death of Christ is an unrepeatable historical event. It is, therefore, often suggested that the saving events have affected the heavenly existence of the Lord and are "preserved" in his glorified body—so, for instance, H. Kuhaupt, *Die Feier der Eucharistie*, I (Münster, 1950, esp. pp. 115-21). But if one takes seriously the reality of the cult-symbolic manifestation, no such speculation is necessary. The speculation only confuses any attempt to appreciate the true New Testament soteriological perspective in which salvation is achieved through participation in Christ's saving death. Our understanding of sacramental real symbolism, on the other hand, while preserving and emphasizing the uniqueness of the historical death on the cross without suggesting that it is being repeated, does present a kind of "epiphany" (cf. J. M. R. Tillard, "L'Eucharistie et le Saint Ésprit," in *Nouv. Rev. Théol.* 100 [1968], p. 385), in which the death becomes really and effectively present for those who perform the symbolic rite in faith and let it affect themselves. Apart from the fact that the Christ event has an "eschatological" character in virtue of which it surpasses temporal boundaries and possesses the power to draw all things to itself (see esp. Jn. 12, 31f.), we for our part must fulfill two conditions in order to encounter the dying Lord in person: (1) we must perform the sacramental symbolism through which the saving deed is objectively and effectively made accessible and (2) we must believe and so be enabled to see the true significance of this symbol, to be lifted in a real spiritual fashion beyond the bounds of space and time and to share in this saving event sacramentally made manifest. Most difficulties with the "mystery presence" come from those bound by Aristotelian presuppositions as to the nature of time in agreement neither with those of the Bible nor with modern science (time as relative and not an absolute!) and useless when it comes to discuss the spiritual actions in saving

these texts to conceive of baptism as a true cult mystery without compromising genuine Christian experience by drawing unnecessarily upon heathen ideas. This cult mystery does not cause a new saving act of Christ to occur or recur; rather it causes this one act to achieve a new symbolic or sacramental and real presence, so that by accepting and sharing it and its effects, in faith, we can obtain some participation of the salvation achieved by Christ. The foundation, continuance and realization of the salvation of the redeemed necessarily include a share in the existence and fate of the redeemer. The source of this understanding lies in the ancient biblical doctrine of the solidarity that exists between people both in guilt and also in salvation (esp. Heb. 2, 10-18).

3. Real Image and Real Presence in the Eucharist

The eucharist also can be conceived of as a *homoioma* or cultic image which is as full of reality as is its source. If this expression was not directly used of the eucharist in the New Testament, it was so used very soon after.[8] The references in the early eucharistic consecratory prayers (the *Quam oblationem* of the Roman canon, for instance) to the *similitudo* or the *figura corporis et sanguinis Domini* imply no weakening of the order of reality; the inference is rather—in line with the ancient conception of an *eikon*—that the reality is present in the image.

The New Testament itself gives no cause to doubt the reality of the presence of Christ in the sacrament; on the contrary it

---

history. The biblical understanding of time makes pointless any recourse to the "now" of the glorified Lord in heaven in order to justify the sacramental real presence of his saving death. This is not to deny that the Lord is present and active through his Spirit in the sacrament, but his presence is of one who has achieved new life (the Pasch) through death. This is the nature of our redeemer; his glorification is only the fruit of his sacrificial suffering and not the ground of our redemption. Only by dying with him can we make living contact with the Lord. The reality of the "paschal mystery" depends precisely on the presence in the sacrament of Christ's unique *transitus*. See also notes 14 and 15 below.

[8] For example in Serapion's *Euchologion* (3,12; 3,14; and cf. 4,15) and in the *Prex eucharistica,* ed. A. Hänggi and I. Pahl (Fribourg/ Switz., 1968), pp. 130-1.

provides quite sufficient foundation for that belief. Even apart from the very clear witness of Paul and John which we have mentioned earlier, a critical analysis of the four accounts of the words of institution shows that on both contextual and theological grounds the texts demand a realistic understanding.[9] They imply that the Lord is really and truly present under the appearances of bread and wine in accordance with the teaching of ecclesial tradition, the official declarations of Lateran IV and Trent, down to the present day.[10]

The real presence of Christ in the eucharist ought not to be considered in an isolated or static fashion, as frequently happens. If we are to achieve a deeper insight into its significance the real presence must be seen as related to the events and meaning of saving history. It is the actual presence of the saving work of Christ which substantiates the real presence in this sacrament. Unless accepted as mystery, the eucharist as the real presence is a holy but static affair, an "object" of adoration, rather than a living achievement in which we cooperate and in which we can actively share.[11]

[9] P. Neuenzeit, *Das Herrenmahl. Studien zur paulinischen Eucharistieauffassung* (Munich, 1960), pp. 59f.; 175-83. J. Betz, "Eucharistie," in *Handbuch theol. Grundbegriffe*, I (1962), pp. 338-40. A. Stöger, "Eucharistie," in *Bibeltheol. Wörterbuch* (1967³), pp. 356-8; 362.

[10] Only the most recent pronouncements are noted here. When Pope Paul VI had finished summarizing the *Constitution on the Liturgy* of Vatican II (n. 7) on the different modes of the eucharistic presence of Christ, he states of this that it is real *per excellentiam, quia est substantialis, qua nimirum totus atque integer Christus, Deus et homo, fit praesens (Mysterium Fidei, A.A.S.* (1965), p. 764. See also the *Instructio de cultu mysterii eucharistici* of May 25, 1967, n.1; A. Piolanti, "I motivi dell'Enciclica 'Mysterium Fidei' ", in *Divinitas*, 10 (1966), pp. 237-71; E. Gutwenger, "Das Geheimnis der Gegenwart Christi in der Eucharistie," in *ZkTh*, 88 (1966), pp. 185-97; E. Schillebeeckx, *Die eucharistische Gegenwart. Zur Diskussion über die Realpräsenz* (Düsseldorf, 1967) (Note: this is the German translation of essays written principally in Dutch in various publications. See: "Transubstantiation, Transfinalization, Transfiguration" in *Worship* (June, 1966), pp. 324-38 for a sample in English); W. Beinert, "Die Enzyklika 'Mysterium Fidei' und neuer Auffassungen über Eucharistie," in *Theol. Quartalschrift*, 147 (1967), pp. 159-76. The *Credo* which Paul VI promulgated on June 30, 1968 also has strong emphasis on the real presence of Christ in the eucharist.

[11] The *"actuosa participatio"* which Pius XI and Pius XII had already

The analogy with the Pauline understanding of baptism will already have suggested to us that there is a real presence of the saving work of Christ in the eucharist. Paul, in connection with the eucharist, does in fact emphasize that in the eucharistic meal we "announce the death of the Lord until he comes" (1 Cor. 11, 26). This announcement (*katangellein*), most will admit today, is the proclamation: an event which actually happens. The memorial character of the Lord's supper (*loc. cit.*, 11, 24f.; see Lk. 22, 19), because of its direct (or at least indirect) relationship to the paschal meal, also suggests the presence of the saving reality, for the Jews recognized in the remembrance of the Pasch that they had a real share in the events through which their people were freed from slavery in Egypt. Consequently if the cultic celebration of the eucharist makes the saving work present [12] then the Savior himself must also be really present for the event itself cannot be personified (or petrified) on its own.

---

much emphasized was emphatically underlined by the *Constitution on the Liturgy* of Vatican II (n. 48). For the whole subject see especially J. Betz, "Eucharistie", in *LThK* [2] III (1959), cols 1156f.

[12] The phrase in the Secret prayer of the 9th Sunday after Pentecost: *quoties huius hostiae commemoratio celebratur, opus nostrae redemptionis exercetur*, at least in its *sensus obvius*, provides support if anything for Casel's mystery doctrine, despite the contrary interpretation by W. Diezinger, *Effectus in der römischen Liturgie* (Bonn, 1961), pp. 137-46; compare Vatican II's *Constitution on the Church* I, n. 3.: *Quoties sacrificium crucis . . . in altari celebratur, opus nostrae redemptionis exercetur*. On the difficulties thus raised see J. Betz, "Die Gegenwart der Heilstat Christi", in *Wahrheit und Verkündigung* (Festschrift for M. Schmaus, Paderborn, 1967), pp. 1807-26, esp. pp. 1813f.; J. A. Jungmann, *Liturgisches Erbe und pastorale Gegenwart* (Innsbruck, 1960) p. 507. The close connections between the mystery presence and the real presence (or transubstantiation) were underlined by O. Casel in his posthumous work: *Das christliche Opfermysterium* (Graz, 1968), pp. 464-6, 469-81, etc. which the present writer edited. On this point the most recent essay is O. Hagemeyer, "Ökumenisches Gaspräch über die Realpräsenz", in *Erbe u. Auftrag* 44 (1968), pp. 317-24. The essay corrects the view of the reformed theologian J. Plooij in his otherwise very scholarly work, *De Mysterie-Leer van Odo Casel. Een bijdrage tot het oecumenisch gesprek der Kerken* (Zwolle, 1964; German translation by O. Hagemeyer, Neustadt a. cl. Aich., 1968), that the mystery doctrine made the "theory" of transubstantiation superfluous.

Not even the Church is an adequate subject of the saving events of the sacrifice of the Mass for she, too, is among the redeemed. The saving work must always be Christ's, his personal act. Hence, the "substantial" or "personal" presence of Christ in the sacrament is demanded and supported by the mystery presence.

Further support for this is to be seen in the well-founded scriptural doctrine [13] that the eucharistic celebration is a sacrificial action. True, this sacrifice can save and redeem only insofar as it is one with the sole valid and unique new covenant, the sacrifice which atones for all. If the Mass is to be a true sacrifice identical with the unique sacrifice of the cross then the one offered on the cross and the gifts he offered (that is, the flesh and blood of Christ which are the symbols of his self-offering) must be present at Mass though of course without their historical circumstances. The real presence is therefore related in the first place to the crucified Lord; or better, to the one who dies on the cross and so enters into his glory. His body is present, being "offered for you" (Lk. 22, 19; see 1 Cor. 11, 24) here and now, and his blood is now being "shed for you", "shed for many", (Mk. 14, 24; Mt. 26, 28; Lk. 22, 20).[14] The sacrifice of Christ

[13] On the discussion about the sacrificial character of the last supper in recent evangelical literature see W. Averbeck, *Den Opfercharakter des Abendmahls in der neueren evangelischen Literatur* (Paderborn, 1967). O. Casel (*op. cit.* pp. 70-98, and frequently, see index of contents) has emphasized that the Mass is also the sacrifice of the Church; see also Ch. V. Héris, *L'Eucharistie mystère de foi* (Colmar and Paris, 1967), pp. 187-216. The "Letter from the German bishops to all those who are entrusted by the Church with preaching the faith" of Dec. 1, 1967 (n. 40) says that the Mass has its sacrificial character in virtue of the sacramental presence of the sacrifice of the cross; see B. Schlindwein, "Zur Diskussion über die Eucharistie", in *Theologie der Gegenwart* 11 (1968), p. 88. The unity of meal and sacrifice in the eucharistic celebration indicated in the *Constitution on the Sacred Liturgy* (n. 47) is clearly stated in *Mysterium Fidei* (*loc. cit.*, 754, 762), and in the *Instructio* referred to in note 10 (n. 3); on this see J. Ratzinger, "Is the Eucharist a Sacrifice?", in Concilium 24 (1967); A. Winklhofer, *Kirche in den Sakramenten* (Frankfurt, 1968), pp. 67-89; also the Dutch catechism, *A New Catechism. Catholic Faith for Adults* (London and New York, 1967) esp. p. 339f.

[14] According to the mystery presence doctrine the *participia praesentia* in the words of institution do not need to be understood in a future sense

on the cross is both the *kairos* which fulfills all time and removes temporal boundaries, and also a definitive call to choose (*krisis* Jn. 12, 31). If we wish to be saved we must enter into this *kairos,* which as an "eschatological event" breaks the bonds of time and is therefore accessible to all ages. We encounter it concretely in the Word and sacraments: first in preaching and baptism, and then continually in the eucharist, until we finally "sleep with Christ" and share in his own last exodus (1 Cor. 15, 18; see 1 Thess. 4, 14-16).

We do not want to suggest that the glorified Lord is not also present in the eucharist. He is in fact the goal of the eucharistic event. However, it is its Easter character which determines this aspect. In it the paschal mystery confronts us in a concrete cult symbol.[15] We have already shared in this mystery in baptism and must continue to live it until the *parousia,* be this our own death or the end of the world. From this stems both the seriousness and the joy that should mark every eucharistic celebration.

---

since even at the last supper his sacrifice on the cross was present to the Lord in anticipation. In any case the *Instructio de cultu mysterii eucharistici* (n. 3b) is certainly correct when it says: *Participatio vero Coenae dominicae semper est communio cum Christo sese Patri pro nobis in sacrificium offerente.* But the phrase in n. 1 seems to contradict this when it says that the gifts in the eucharist *in Corpus et Sanguinem gloriosum convertuntur* (n. 1). However, these only reflect the two different ways we have of viewing the paschal mystery: from our own historical existence we meet the crucified Christ, but from "above" we meet the glorified Lord: "The risen one who comes close to us through his cross" (W. Hahn, *Gottesdienst und Opfer Christi* [Göttingen 1951], p. 67). The body of the crucified Lord is our redemptive sacrifice, the body of the risen Lord is our food. Because he has this spiritual mode of existence he is *able* to be present everywhere; but he is not so present automatically, as also *Mysterium Fidei* states (*loc. cit.,* p. 764), but only through the performance of the eucharistic mystery.

15 According to A. Winklhofer (*op. cit.,* p. 294) the content of the phrase "paschal mystery" comes from O. Casel; on this see note 46 in our introduction to the book: *Das christliche Opfermysterium.* Apart from the literature quoted there, see also J. M. R. Tillard, *The Eucharist, Pasch of God's People* (Staten Island, 1967); E. Gutwenger, "Pascha-Mysterium und Eucharistie", in *ZkTh* 89 (1967), pp. 339-46. See also note 7 above.

4. The Transformation at the Consecration

The real symbol, whose roots in sacred history we have indicated, leads us to a greater understanding of the mystery of the eucharist. Not only the eucharistic gifts but also the sacred actions are symbols in the strict sense, for the reality symbolized is actually present in both.[16]

If we start with the eucharistic event we can see there, as in all cultic sacrifices, a process that has three phases: gifts are brought or offered, they are set apart for God and they are consecrated for his acceptance. Corresponding to these three cult acts there are the three existential "moments": the self-offering (renunciation), the transformation (movement from the profane to the sacred realm), and the union with God (communion).[17] The bread and wine in the eucharist are offered, therefore, as signs of our own self-offering. As such they already have a symbolic value in their own right, if only in a very preliminary sense. The sacrifice of the Mass does not really consist of our gifts or self-offering; rather both are symbols through which the sacrifice of Christ accomplishes itself. What we have to offer, however valuable and noble, can never effect salvation and sanctification. We are expected to offer gifts and, above all, ourselves,[18] but these

[16] The word "actio" whose cultic significance O. Casel first drew attention to ("Actio in liturgischer Verwendung", in *Jahrb. f. Liturgiewiss.*, 1 [1921], pp. 34-9) is met with also in the *Instructio* mentioned in note 10 (n. 3c) and quite generally in theological literature including the Letter of the German bishops (n. 40) mentioned in note 13.

[17] On this point see our work on religious phenomenology: *Vom Wesen des kultischen Opfers*, in *Opfer Christi und Opfer der Kirche*, ed. B. Neunheuser (Düsseldorf, 1960), pp. 29-74, esp. pp. 61-5.

[18] Even M. Luther had allowed this in a qualified sense, see V. Warnach, "Das Meßopfer als ökumenisches Anliegen", in *Lit. u. Möncht.* 17 (1955), pp. 66-9; H. B. Meyer, *Luther und die Messe* (Paderborn, 1965), pp. 137-72. The "crisis" among theologians trying to understand the Offertory makes them tend to reduce its significance, or even to eliminate it altogether (see the Dutch Catechism referred to in note 13, pp. 335, 340). Although it is no autonomous unit, but only preparatory to the eucharistic celebration, bread and wine are offered so that they may be changed into the body and blood of Christ (N.M.Denis-Boulet, *Analyse des rites et des prières de la Messe*, in *L'église en prière*, ed. A. G. Martimort (Paris, 1965³), pp. 377f.; nevertheless, the offering

are useless if they do not become part of Christ's sacrifice. Though it is God who invites us to offer gifts, it is he alone who, through the Spirit of Christ, sanctifies and consecrates them. Our offerings are themselves God's gift to us and so must always become thanksgiving (*eucharistia*) for these offerings and for all the works of creation and salvation.

This thanksgiving "in the name of Jesus" is the efficacious word which transforms and consecrates the offerings—it "eucharistizes" them as Justin said.[19] They then become *symbola,* visible manifestations of the sanctified body and blood of the crucified Christ. The unique saving sacrifice becomes a saving and sanctifying presence among us.

The Mass is not *just* a sacrificial action, it is also a sacrificial *meal.* That is why we offer food. But this food now has a very different meaning. It functions not just to nourish and strengthen man's body so that he can prolong his earthly life, but principally to feed the "inner man", not just his "soul" but the whole of his human nature so as to prepare him for the "other" true eternal life with God.

There is therefore at least a threefold change in the fundamental significance of the bread and wine: (1) prior to the consecration they function as signs of our self-offering; after it they realize the presence in a symbol of Christ's sacrifice on the cross; (2) bread and wine become more than purely natural nourish-

---

belongs to the unified structure of the Mass (J. A. Jungmann, *op. cit.,* p. 367f.; Th. Schnitzler, *Der römische Meβkanon* (Freiburg i. Br., 1968), pp. 29-31, cf. pp. 88f.). On the meaning of the Offertory: W. J. Grisbrooke, "Oblation at the Eucharist", in *Studia liturg.* 3 (1964), pp. 227-39; 4 (1965) pp. 37-55; A. M. Argenti, "El ofertorio en la celebracion de la eucaristia", in *Phase* 6 (1966), pp. 391-402; G. Oury, "La significa-tion de l'offertoire", in *Ami du clergé* 76 (1966), pp. 362-6. Even evangelical theologians speak of the sacrificial offering of the Church, for instance, M. Thurian, *L'Eucharistie* (Neuchâtel-Paris 1963²), and the recent work by H. Asmussen, *Christliche Lehre anstatt eines Katechismus* (Berlin-Hamburg, 1968), p. 108f; further references in W. Averbeck, *op. cit.,* note 13, esp. p. 785.

[19] Justin, *Apol.* I, 65. 67; cf. Irenaeus, *Adv. haer.* V, 2. 3; on this see O. Casel, *Das christliche Opfermysterium* (Graz, 1968), pp. 114f, 293-7, 315ff, 389-92, 395ff; and also J. Pascher, *Eucharistia* (Münster-Freiburg i. Br., 1953²), p. 122f.

ment; they are "spiritual food" (1 Cor. 10, 3); (3) as part of a meal they constitute a table-fellowship among those present, but in communion the eucharistic gifts unite us first to Christ, then through him with one another in the one spiritual body of the Church. These transignifications, to which can be linked a radical transfinalization and a transfunctionalization, do not explain the totality of the eucharistic mystery; they do not even represent the full riches of the teaching to be found in both Scripture and tradition. They are inadequate of themselves correctly to account for the eucharistic event even if "significance" should mean nature, for more than nature (= contents) is at stake here; we are concerned with *being* [20] as well.

If we try to situate the eucharist within saving history we perceive that it is the meeting place of the descent (*katabasis*) of the self-emptying (*kenosis*) and the ascent (*anabasis*) to glorification (*doxa*). To be more precise: the paschal mystery is realized in the eucharist to the extent that it also contains that unique *kairos*, that irrevocable all-embracing turning point in Christ's course through his sacrificial death to a new life. The path which stretches from his incarnation to the criminal's death on a cross is expressed in the sacrament by him, emptying himself under the forms of bread and wine, so that the eucharist can be valued as a new incarnation of Christ. Its meaning stems from the "perpetuation" [21] of his unique sacrifice and from the fellowship (*koinonia*) of the sacred meal.

The natural creative power of selfless love changes the earthly materials of bread and wine in their innermost being, making them like a window through which shines the self-offering and glorification of the dying and risen Lord—visible to those with faith. Just as Jesus' visible body was his historical and personal manifestation (*species*) in his temporal existence, so the euchar-

[20] The ontological aspect, which acording to E. Schillebeeckx "is undoubtedly an object of faith and not just a manner of expression" (*op. cit.*, note 22, p. 54) has been underlined especially by *Mysterium Fidei*, (*loc. cit.*, pp. 766, 764f).

[21] See the same encyclical, p. 754, where it follows the *Constitution on the Liturgy* (n. 47). This word is not to be understood in a static sense, but in a dynamic one within the context of saving history.

istic gifts are the manifestation (*species*) of Christ in his transition to the world of God. We, too, must share in this unique transition if we wish to be saved.

Although we can parallel the "form" of bread and wine and the human form of the "fleshly body" (Col. 1, 22), there are nevertheless essential differences between the historical and the sacramental manifestations of Christ: (1) the body which the *Logos* took from the Virgin is only a "symbol" for the present Lord in a derivative sense, whereas the bread and wine, because of their institution and consecration, are proper cult symbols and consequently make him present; (2) the presence of Christ in the sacrament is not historical or spatio-temporal but real and "substantial" (or better, personal) which as sacramental or pneumatic is beyond space and time, as the encyclical *Mysterium Fidei* emphasized.[22] This spiritual or pneumatic form of

[22] So we have on p. 762: *per consecrationis verba (Dominus) sacramentaliter incipit praesens adesse . . . sub speciebus panis et vini.* This seems to be contradicted when it says later on: *sub quibus (speciebus) totus et integer Christus adest in sua physica "realitate" etiam corporaliter praesens, licet non eo modo quo corpora sunt in loco* (p. 766). But this only emphasizes the "bodily" reality of the presence of the Lord in a context where the non-spatial manner of the Lord's bodily presence is being emphasized. Even Thomas taught this: the body of Christ in the eucharist is *nullo modo . . . localiter* present *sed per modum substantiae* (S. T. III, 76, 5) or more precisely: *non per modum corporis, id est, prout est in sua specie visibili* but *prout est spiritualiter, id est, invisibili modo, et virtute spiritus* (*op. cit.*, 75, 1 *ad* 4). We can take as our basic assumption that the same (personal) body of Christ is: the "fleshly body" (Col. 1, 22, cf. 2, 11) of his earthly existence; the glorified (*doxa*, Phil. 3, 21) or "spiritual body" (1 Cor. 15, 44) in heaven; the "one body in Christ" (Rom. 12, 5) of the Church; and the body under the appearances of bread and wine; all these are different analogous manifestations of the same reality (see note 14 above). Consequently, one can say of the eucharistic mode of presence that it is neither physical and sensual, nor a material object, nor purely symbolic and abstract, nor just spiritual, but a real or sacramental symbol in that it manifests a spiritual (pneumatic) or personal reality to the believer through visible forms as a living and a life-giving presence. It cannot be separated from the cultic sacrifice and meal which the Church celebrates, and so from the spiritual and personal presence of the Lord working in her, himself present through his Spirit and his Word in the gifts, offering himself in the sacrifice and meal and enabling us to share in these. One can only quote from the immense literature on this: E. Schillebeeckx, *Die eucharistische Gegenwart* (full

existence is not less real but rather more fully real. In contrast to an impoverished and empty idea of reality to be found in positivism, Christian realism has always seen in spiritual being its highest and richest form, positively surpassing space and time by overflowing their boundaries. Matter is not thereby denied value or turned into spirit. It is illumined and made radiant through the spirit, brought to its true fulfillment in the unity and completeness (*pleroma*) of Christ's spiritual body. So our sacrificial gifts undergo a radical (ontological) transformation which leaves their form (species) unaltered as the manifesting medium, while radically altering their being, giving them totally new relationships and connections.

What we mean can be clarified and to some extent justified by a short consideration of the fundamental ontological structure of things. Modern science and scientifically orientated philosophy considers bread and wine to be a mixture of organic and inorganic materials which cannot properly speaking be called "substances" (that is, entities relatively independent in their own being but not their origin). The true substance of bread and wine is rather the cosmos "not yet as" a system of purely physical forces and fields but as the nature (*physis*) transformed by man.

Bread and wine represent together, in a picture, a world fashioned by human resources. They are especially suitable therefore to symbolize (in a broad sense) human self-offering. They are the principal materials by which men are nourished and they imply man's limitation to this world. Naturally they are typical of human offerings since Melchizedek's time, if not long before that.

In the present saving order our human offerings become meaningless unless they are part of the one saving sacrifice of

---

details in note 10) and the review by J. Ratzinger in *ThQ* 147 (1967), pp. 493-6. For what follows see L. Scheffczyk, "Die materielle Welt im Lichte der Eucharistie", in *Aktuelle Fragen zur Eucharistie*, ed. M. Schmaus (Munich, 1960), pp. 156-79, and B. Welte's supplement on pp. 190-5, but noting that both authors proceed from ontological presuppositions different from ours.

Christ. He has therefore taken our useless gifts and made them his own, his own sacrifice of body and blood, thus linking them with his very being which is by nature one of sacrificial love. In this way they are changed ontologically and become the "species" of a different "substance".[23] The ground and the meaning of their being, that is, their "substance" is no longer the cosmos; it is Christ himself, the Lord of the cosmos, who makes these "forms" (*species*) into a self-manifestation.[24] Bread and wine, therefore, become his body and blood; through them he really and sacramentally "appears", offering himself here and now. The cult-symbol finds in this rite its highest realization. In this sense one can really speak of "transubstantiation", meaning that instead of the substance of the cosmos Christ himself bears bread and wine as his "species", so that they express him and he becomes their "substance".

Linked to this transubstantiation there are also a transfunctionalization, transignification and transfinalization which affect

[23] The philosophical term, "substance", (or "substantial") is often used in the sense of "nature" (*essentia, ousia*), or even in contrast to these latter to mean "subject" (*subiectum, hypokeimenon*), a usage which stems from Aristotelian usage. Consequently, the eucharistic event was described in the 12th century, and especially by Petrus Cantor, as a change of subject, that is, as a change in the (bodily) material (as distinct from the *forma materialis*) (S. H. Jorissen, *Die Entfaltung der Transsubstantiationslehre bis zum Beginn der Hochscholastik* [Munster, 1965], pp. 87-114), while one often translated transubstantiation into the German *"Wesensverwandlung"* (change of nature) as does also L. Scheffczyk (*op. cit.*, p. 168-70). It is our opinion, however, that what is affected here is not the subject (bearer) or the nature (contents) as such, but rather being which unites bearer and contents. It is in this sense that we speak of substance as the true or independent existent. It is here that we agree with the modern tendency to regard the substance of the eucharist as a person, or at least as personal; see for instance E. Schillebeeckx, *op. cit.*, pp. 47f., 53f.; J. Ratzinger, "Das Problem der Transsubstantiation und die Frage nach dem Sinn der Eucharistie", in *ThQ* 147 (1967), p. 152.

[24] The eucharistic change can be compared with the "transfiguration" of Christ on Tabor where the glorified Christ also appeared in *altera specie* (Lk. 9, 29; cf. 3, 22). J. M. R. Tillard (*op. cit.*, note 7) has very clearly shown that the Spirit was at work in this change even though he does tend to enhance the role of the Spirit as the third person of the Trinity in contrast to that of the Spirit of Christ, to the neglect of the important role of the latter in saving history.

the depths of reality in the offerings; bread and wine are no longer the manifestation of a civilized world, but a manifestation of Christ. They no longer function to support man's earthly life but support the new life in the Spirit. Their goal is no longer to foster the growth of a community around a table but to unite man with Christ and with all who are in him. "Whoever eats my flesh and drinks my blood abides in me and I in him" (Jn. 6, 56).

The breath of Christ's Spirit and the power of the words of institution uttered in the place of, and in the name of, the Lord cause this penetrating change. "This (bread belonging to this cosmos) is (from now on supported and informed by Christ as) my body," that is, as an expression of the being of the Lord himself in a cult-symbolic manifestation.

We can hardly visualize or even guess what it really means to say that a piece of bread manifests not the cosmos but the incarnate God. This is not a denial or destruction of its being but raises it to a new level of existence. Bread and wine are "first fruits" of the cosmos, consecrated to God, changed through the powerful consecration of the Spirit. They are raised up by Christ to be himself, to become his "ambassadors" in this material world and so to receive a divine value. The eucharistic figures represent the Lord in bodily form in a manner analogous to that in which his physical body expressed him. But these things are also chosen in the sense that they anticipate something that one day will be shared by the whole cosmos.

The radical nature of the transformation by no means implies any questioning of the *personal* presence of Christ in the eucharistic mystery.[25] Any complete biblical ontology understands that

[25] In line with our discussion of terminology in note 23, this is equivalent to *conversio totius entis, ut scilicet tota substantia huius convertatur in totam substantiam illius* which is St. Thomas' understanding of the doctrine of transubstantiation (*S.T.* III, 75, 4) or to *conversio totius substantiae panis in corpus (Christi)* . . . which is how *Mysterium Fidei* puts it. Even E. Schillebeeckx talks of a "change of being" which he characterizes as a "sacramental parousia" (*op. cit.*, p. 55). Our own interpretation follows that of the Greek Fathers according to whom Christ takes the bread and wine for his own property in order to manifest him-

true being is personal, though always directed toward the community and only fully realized in it. Hence, the eucharist is also an eminently social sacrament, or in more concrete terms an *ecclesial* sacrament. And it is this in two senses: it forms the community (1 Cor. 10, 16f.), and it demands brotherly love of members of the community. The Church is both of, and for, the world in the eucharistic meal/sacrifice, without being worldly herself. She would have nothing to give the world and could not be the "sign lifted up among the nations" that Vatican II announced to be her true mission if she were ever to become worldly.[26]

Yet the eucharist is not an *experimentum rationis* but a *mysterium fidei*. What happens in it is experienced only in faith, that is, the continued incarnation of Christ in a sacred meal and his offering of himself in the sacrifice which changes and perfects all things.

5. Anticipated Eschatology

Let us penetrate a little further by considering the "ultimate mystery". The predominantly concrete reality of the sacrament of the eucharist is more than a symbol containing the reality of an (historical) act of God from the past; it is also a type of what is to come, the final realization of God's all-embracing kingdom (*basileia*). The eucharist is no terminus, but a beginning and a pledge of future perfection: *pignus puturae gloriae*. Like every sacrifice, the Mass involves a transformation and translation of

---

self in them, to reincarnate himself in them; on this see J. Betz, *Die Eucharistie in der Zeit der griechischen Väter* I/1 (Freiburg i. Br., 1955), pp. 300-18; see also E. Schillebeeckx, *op. cit.*, pp. 43ff., where the author speaks, however, of a de-substantatio since bread and wine are falsely conceived of as substances. On this problem see also P. Schoonenberg, "Transubstantiation: How Far Is This Doctrine Historically Determined?", in *Concilium* 24 (1967).

[26] Since we cannot go into the personal and ecclesial aspects of the eucharistic mystery here, the reader is referred to our book: *Agape, Die Liebe als Grundmotiv neutestamentlicher Theologie* (Dusseldorf, 1951), esp. pp. 215-371, 550-640; see also "L'Eglise comme mystère, comme sacrement, come Communion," in *La nouvelle image de l'Eglise* (Paris, 1967), pp. 39-65.

something from the profane to the sacred realm. It transcends this world and is therefore quite correctly called an eschatological event. It does more than "announce the death of Christ until he comes again" (1 Cor. 11, 26); in some ways it anticipates this advent and presages the messianic banquet in heaven. At least this was the way in which the early Christians understood it.

We have already remarked that the transformed gifts are "first fruits" not only of what is past but also of the future age. The change in the bread and wine anticipates that in which all things will share at the end of the world. They are to be transformed into a spiritual-pleromic being and will be incorporated into the spiritual (because glorified) body of the Lord.

At the advent (*parousia*) of Christ in which all things will be fulfilled he will manifest and complete his "birth into the eternal now" through the Father, as Acts 13, 33 suggests. On the other hand, the primitive Christian hymn Paul hands on in Colossians 1, 15-20 supposes an eternal incarnation prior to the historical incarnation from Mary. This hymn says of Christ (that is, of the incarnate *Logos*) that he is the "firstborn of all creation" through whom and for whom all things have been created and in whom "all things subsist" (protologically and eschatologically have their "substance"). As not a few early Church theologians taught, this incarnation of Christ before time must be closely connected with the primordial expression of the creative words. In this way all creation is conceived of as the explication of Christ's humanity.[27] To this development (*explicatio*) of the primal word of creation there corresponds the final return (*reditio*) of all creation through Christ to its origin in the Father. But since this eternal decree of God (which is the prime mystery) is that "in the fullness of time everything that is in heaven and on earth should be gathered together again in Christ as its head" (Eph. 1, 9f), this return to unity (*anakephalaiosis, redin-*

---

[27] For the biblical and patristic background to this theologoumenon see our book: *Das Christusmysterium. Ein Entwurf der Mysterientheologie nach dem Neuen Testament.* The work, completed in 1941 but not yet published owing to unfavorable circumstances, is to be published soon by the Patmos-Verlag in Düsseldorf. See esp. section II, 5.

tegratio) also incorporates all things into the body of Christ—a spiritual body that includes all things because it penetrates beyond the bounds of space and time. It is the birth of the "whole Christ" in the eternal Christmas.

The eucharist is in some senses the apex of this immense process of the incorporation and the spiritualization of the world in Christ "through the eternal Spirit" (cf. Heb. 9, 14). For it realizes already in its real symbolism that universal and total "transubstantiation" by which Christ will be the "substance" of all things and so will replace the cosmos. It is he who "through the word (*rhema*) of his power supports all things" (Heb. 1, 3), and who is also the "primal symbol" *par excellence,* being the "expression (*charakter*) of the substance (*hypostasis*)" of God.[28]

A correct understanding of symbol helps protect us here from monism or pantheism. The created world is not Christ inasmuch as he is God but is his "body", that is, his real symbolical manifestation or (in the *parousia*) his radiant glorification. On the other hand, the love (*agape*) which first and last has characterized the events in this world demands and makes possible, as does all personal love, the greatest union between those who love and gives them also the greatest freedom. Quite apart from the cosmic implications, the eschatological event is through and through personal; it is the solemn thanksgiving (*eucharistia*) which Christ utters to the Father by bringing back to him a redeemed creation made perfect through the Spirit (cf. 1 Cor. 15, 24). The deepest impulse and real purpose for going out from God and returning to him is love—that love by which Christ has become man and flesh, a sacrifice and food for us. Hence, he "fills all in all" through the Church (Eph. 1, 23), so that God himself may be "all in all" (1 Cor. 15, 28).

In this necessarily brief account I hope to have shown not only what in the mind of Councils and the constant official teaching is the deeper significance of the eucharist, but also to have related

[28] On this see K. Rahner, *On the Theology of the Symbol,* in *Theological Investigations* IV, (London and Baltimore, 1966), pp. 239f.

this doctrine within the framework of God's general providence (*oikonomia*). Here the concept of real symbol plays an important and illuminating role, significant for a correct Christian understanding of the world, of creation and redemptive history, of protology as well as eschatology. The eucharistic mystery so concentrates concretely within itself God's ways of dealing with men that it must be held to be the true source and center of Christian living. It is in the fullest sense of the words the *sacramentum unitatis* whose significance for a mankind struggling for universal *unity* is not less decisive because it has become the more neglected.

Josef Ernst/*Paderborn, West Germany*

Significance of Christ's Eucharistic Body for the Unity of Church and Cosmos

R ecent theological scholarship has again shown a marked tendency to maintain that the very remarkable idea of the "body of Christ" found in the Pauline letters has its source in a realistic and physical kind of union with Christ such as takes place in the sacramental events of baptism and the eucharist and has found verbal expression in the "In Christ" formula.[1] In virtue of the *Pneuma,* the one crucified body of Jesus Christ becomes present in the bread of the Lord's supper. By eating this one bread, the many once more make a reality of what they already are: "one body" (1 Cor. 10, 17). The "communion" of this body with the exalted Christ (1 Cor. 10, 16) requires the constant actualization of Jesus' diaconia, for it thus to become "one body in Christ" (Rom. 12, 5) and "the body of Christ" which "has built itself up in love" (Eph. 4, 16) and attains "to the measure of the stature of the fullness of Christ" (Eph. 4, 13). This growth of the body to Christ its head also operates with saving effect for the cosmos, which in and with the

---

[1] P. Benoit, "Head and Pleroma in the Epistles of the Captivity," in *Exégèse et dogmatique* first published in *Revue biblique* 63 (1956), pp. 5-44; *Exegese und Theologie* (Düsseldorf, 1965), pp. 246-79, especially pp. 248-52. Previously, by A. E. J. Rawlinson, *"Corpus Christi,"* in *Mysterium Christi,* edited by G. K. A. Bell; and A. Deibmann (Berlin, 1931), pp. 275-95. Tr. Schmidt, *Der Leib Christi, Eine Untersuchung zum urchristlichen Gemeindegedanken* (Leipzig, 1919), pp. 206-9.

Church is drawn into the work of redemption and attains the *pleroma*. The point at which this meeting of Church and cosmos, order of creation and order of redemption, takes place even now, is the celebration of the eucharist. Consequently the Pauline metaphor of the body, and of the body of Christ, with its social, ecclesial, christological, soteriological and cosmological implications, indubitably has its center in this sacramental, eucharistic foundation, and on this basis it is susceptible of a single, coherent interpretation.

1. *The Real Union with Christ of the Eucharistic Meal as the Foundation of the Social Community of the "One Body"*

The meaning of the extremely important text, 1 Corinthians 10, 16f., is only clear from the context as a whole. Paul is arguing against taking part in pagan sacrificial meals which, according to the ideas of the pagan mystery cults, produced an almost magical identity between the god in whose honor the meal was held and those who ate it. This background clearly explains Paul's intentions. Just as the flesh offered in sacrifice to idols produces a very real union with the idols, so too does the "soma" of the Lord's supper. Paul says: "The bread which we break, is it not a participation (*koinōnia*, i.e., communion) in the body of Christ" (10, 16)? This does not just denote some kind of vaguely idealistic union with Christ, or even merely familiar social companionship at table; it means a real participation in the body of the Lord such as happens when food is ingested. The apostle is not afraid of the danger of possible magical misunderstanding, though of course this is excluded by the term "communion" (*koinōnia*) with its fundamentally personal connotation. At all events "the communion of the body of Christ" brought about by the breaking of the bread cannot be thought of realistically enough; this is also shown by the "baptizing (immersion) into the death of Jesus Christ" (Rom. 6, 3) at baptism, as well as by the comparison with sexual union in marriage (1 Cor. 6, 15). Nor is Pauline pneumatology any argument to the contrary, for it must never be misinterpreted in the sense of Platonist spirituality. The body of the risen Lord is indeed a pneumatic body, but precisely as such is a very real and genuine one. Sacramental union with the body of the crucified and exalted Christ is therefore pneumatic and mystical but precisely as such, real and corporeal.

Christ's individual body is united with those who eat the eucharistic meal and by that very fact unites those who join with Christ in eating the bread and holding the meal into the community of a single body. "Because there is one bread, we who are many are one body, for we all partake of the one bread" (1 Cor. 10, 17). It must therefore be noted here that the expression "the one body which we are" takes on an additional meaning, in the sense of the very close solidarity that binds together those who are united with Christ. The real, pneumatic communion with Christ is the foundation and cause of the "one single body" of the congregation.

It is not easy to grasp and express in words the close connection between the christological-sacramental and the ecclesiological body of Christ. We might speak of two different modes of being of the one body; this is quite correct in itself but would scarcely correspond to the biblical mode of thought. The ancient Church down to Augustine's time used the paraphrase "mystical body" to denote simultaneously and inseparably the eucharistic and the ecclesiological body. The Old Testament and Jewish idea of a "corporate personality", in conjunction with the realistic physical view of the sacraments current in the earliest days of the Church, must have influenced Paul's thought very decisively and led to the use of the idea of the body. At all events these are more likely sources than the Hellenist apologue often cited as a parallel, which compares the State or human society in general to a great all-inclusive body in which the individual members have their special functions. This secular comparison may also have occurred to the apostle while he was composing his letter. But the real origin of the idea is to be sought elsewhere, in the sacramentally represented real body of the crucified and exalted Christ. Understood in this way, the "one body" of 1 Corinthians

10, 17 is more than a metaphor or a metaphorical reality; it is in fact the Lord's own individual body which comprises the bodies of all those who are sacramentally united to him. The sacramentally present body of the crucified and exalted Lord is the "vital space" of those who share in the one bread and are gathered together into a community. Speculative philosophical thought may well experience difficulties here. Paul, however, is thinking christologically and in terms of totality, in line with the primitive Christian view of the "mystical body". After a period of restricted outlook in ecclesiology, greater account is once more being taken of the eucharistic and christological perspectives of that early Christian view. This is certainly to the advantage of a deeper understanding of what the Church essentially is.

The unique character of this community founded in Christ and his real body is primarily explained in 1 Corinthians 12, 27 by baptism. Here, too, however, the power of the eucharist to create and maintain community is not passed over entirely. When in connection with the baptismal event verse 13 speaks of all being "made to drink of one Spirit", we may with Benoit [2] be reminded of "the other great rite of incorporation, the eucharist". But baptism does stand in the foreground as the event which is the foundation of unity. The Christians are "baptized" (i.e. immersed) (13a) into one and the same body. Although the elaborate passage on the charisms and the duty of unity which they entail presents in detail the social implications of the metaphor of the body, and displays clear reminiscences of the well-known Hellenistic apologue, the author even here does not remain on the merely metaphorical level. In verse 27 he draws the conclusion from his teaching and admonitions and says: "Now you are [the] body of Christ and individually members of it." Important here is the expression "body of Christ". The absence of the definite article suggests that in this passage we are not dealing with precisely the same idea of the body of Christ as we find in the letters of the captivity. What is meant is a solidar-

[2] *Op. cit.,* p. 255.

ity with Christ produced by baptism and eucharist and perpetually operative in the *Pneuma* which draws the social structure of that body into the sphere of influence of the *Christ-Pneuma*. Nevertheless the christological orientation must not be overlooked.

Perhaps we should also take into account the conceptual and textual connection with the great adjoining *paraenesis* on love, which describes the origin and vital powers of that body, presenting them in relation to its life. The same link is of course also found in the parallel passage in Romans 12. Here the apostle speaks of "one body in Christ" whose different members are under an obligation to perform various services for the benefit of the whole. It is clearly no accident that this thought is carried further by an appeal for love. The "one body in Christ" is a body imbued with the "dynamis" of Christ; it is within Christ's "sphere of influence".[3] To be in Christ's sphere of influence like this, to be in Christ, also means to be in love. The formulas are equivalent in principle and identical in reality. Love is the essential condition for the actual practice of the various charisms, the ultimate reason for the existence of the one body. Because it is a body "in Christ", it is "in love", and mutual love in the one body takes on a special character through the unique relationship to Christ. At this point it becomes clear that the social aspect of the metaphor of the body is insufficient to explain Pauline thought. In fact it can be said that in the celebration of the Lord's supper the exalted Lord integrates his crucified body, and the love which found free expression in the cross, into his eucharistic body. And since the selfsame body of the exalted Lord is also the ontological ground of his eucharistic and ecclesiological body, his diaconal love is constitutive not only for the eucharist celebration but, precisely through this, for the Church which is "one body". In proportion as the latter participates in the real body of the exalted Christ lovingly offering himself, it becomes "body of Christ", Church, and grows—we may anticipate an idea from the epistles of the captivity—to the head, to Christ. But the force and inspiration of this growth is love (Eph. 4, 16). Thus it is

[3] M. Schmaus, *Katholische Dogmatik* III, 1 (Munich, ³1958), pp. 262f.

clear that love is not only the vital power and origin, but also the vital law of this body. It is therefore advisable to interpret the social element of the solidarity of various members of the community in the one body, both in Romans and 1 Corinthians, in the light of the theme of love which immediately follows. Only if the eucharistic celebration of the Lord's supper is regarded from the point of view of mutual love (cf. 1 Cor. 11, 17ff.), is the eucharistic and ecclesiological body understood in its full reality and depth.

2. *The Unity of the Body of Christ according to the Epistles of the Captivity*

The sacramental foundation and representation of the body of Christ as described in the main Pauline letters with respect to baptism and the eucharist, is also found in the letters of the captivity, though of course from a different angle and in a different light. Here, too, the sequence of thought is traced back to the ultimate source in the actual bodily frame of the redeemer, who sacrificed himself on the cross. All this of course is largely presupposed and is only occasionally mentioned; the immediate focus of attention is the one body formed out of Jews and gentiles (Col. 3, 15; Eph. 2, 16). In this one body Christ established peace between the two hostile groups of mankind. He broke down the dividing wall and reconciled "both to God in one body through the cross, thereby bringing the hostility to an end" (Eph. 2, 16). This one body is the new mankind, whose origin is Christ himself as the "new man" (Eph. 2, 15). In him Jews and gentiles become the one Church. The unifying factor is the sacrifice of the cross; by the blood of his cross (Eph. 2, 13) those "who were far off have been brought near"; by the cross both were reconciled to God (Eph. 2, 16); by it both now have access to the Father (Eph. 2, 18).

The term "body" in the epistles of the captivity expresses the idea of unity, not from the point of view of the individual members who are linked, but in relation to the divided world which is united—this is what is decisive—only by the real sacrificial body of Christ and in such a way as to orientate it toward the one head of all which is Christ. The place in which this unification takes place is baptism, which here is envisaged more specifically in its fundamental salvific value for the Church (cf. Eph. 4, 3f.; Col. 2, 11f.). According to the fifth chapter of Ephesians, Christ gave himself up for his Church in order to sanctify it, by cleansing it "by the washing of water with the word" (5, 26). In this way Christ created unity through the one Spirit. By the mystery of the sacrifice of the cross he "freed", as V. Warnach [4] puts it, his real sacrificial body "from its limits as sarx and transformed it into worldwide pneuma". This pneuma is the "personal sphere" of the glorified Christ, and is identical with being "in Christ".

The Church in the letter to the Ephesians is a reality related to the future aeon; it is the new humanity united by Christ's real sacrificial body. In this way it has become the "body of Christ", the "new man", into which the multitude of Christians have been incorporated in virtue of faith and baptism and are now brought into even greater unity. Here, of course, we must note the danger of metaphysical pantheism which would follow from any inadmissible equation of Christ and Christians. The fact that the real, ontic unity has its root in the personal decision of faith (2, 8), guarantees the necessary difference between head (Christ) and body (community). The "body of Christ" in the letters of the captivity is the body transfigured by death on the cross and resurrection, which by its pneuma-existence is able to draw all believers as members into its personal sphere of life.

The eucharist receives only marginal mention in the perspective of the letters of the captivity. It is the point at which the loving sacrifice of Christ the bridegroom is repeated again and again. When it is said that Christ like a husband nourishes and cherishes the Church as his own flesh (Eph 5, 29), we may probably see this as a reference to the eucharist. It is here regarded less in its constitutive function for the body of Christ than as the domain of loving encounter, bringing life, enlightenment,

---

[4] V. Warnach, (H. Schlier), *Die Kirche im Epheserbrief* (*Beiträge zur Kontroverstheologie* 1) (Münster, 1949), pp. 37ff.

assistance and growth. The eucharist is one of the forces which produce the body's growth toward its head and at the same time perpetually receive their efficacy and vitality from the head. It assists in holding the body together. This circle of ideas is developed in the fourth chapter of Ephesians under various images. According to 4, 16 the whole body is joined and knit together by every joint "of service". This refers to the various ministerial offices which the Lord ascending to heaven gave his Church: apostles, prophets, pastors, teachers who are to build up the body in charity (4, 12. 16). They are to train the saints to carry out their service. It must not be overlooked, then, that official structures of the Church appear here which are, it is true, determined by the idea of service but are nevertheless important in connection with the building up and growth of the body and care for the elements of growth with which Christ has endowed it. Building up and growth take place through the proclamation of the gospel and the mission, but the growth of the body occurs chiefly in the sacraments.

3. *Cosmic Unity in the Body of Christ*

This heading introduces the third aspect of the idea of the body of Christ, its cosmic component. The central thought of bringing together into unity in the body of Christ is extended to all domains of the universe and to God. For this, in the perspective of Ephesians, is the last great goal: to "unite all things" in Christ (1, 10). The world which has disintegrated in sin is to be led back to the center from which its order flows. In Christ, a head is to be given to all things, the cosmos in the widest sense. Christ ascended so that he might fill all things (4, 10). The word "pleroma" used frequently in Ephesians and Colossians, must certainly be regarded as a technical term for this conception. When the letter to the Colossians speaks of the "pleroma" which dwells in Christ, we may possibly, with Benoit,[5] think of the plenitude of God and at the same time of the totality of being which has taken up abode in Christ. Ephesians develops this

[5] *Op. cit.,* p. 273.

thought further. Here the Church is the instrument of the fulfillment of all things. It conveys the powers of healing and redemption even to the non-human realms. The bringing of the cosmos
into the redemptive process takes place through the service of the
Church which as body of Christ is "the fullness of him (i.e.,
Christ) who fills all in all" (Eph. 1, 23). According to the testimony of Ephesians, Church and cosmos are by no means separate, but interrelated. The cosmos can come to fulfillment in
Christ through the Church, just as conversely the Church will
only attain its true pleroma when "the material and non-material
cosmos has been brought into its 'catholic', totally comprehen-
sive unity".[6]

The question is, where and in what way salvation is bestowed
on the cosmic realms. We can probably follow V. Warnach in
attributing an important role to the sacramental process. By baptism, new members are constantly incorporated in the body of
Christ. The eucharist produces the growth of the body toward
the exalted Lord. This of course primarily concerns the domain
of believing humanity united in the Church. But as the Church as
the body of Christ grows in this way toward Christ its head, the
consecratio mundi is taking place. The goal of this process is the
new heaven and the new earth, into which Church and cosmos
both enter. In the sacramental domain of the Church, this goal is
anticipated in sign even now and is effectively pursued. The theological basis here is probably the character of the sacrament as a
symbol-reality. In the symbol of bread, i.e., in a cosmic element,
what is divine is, as it were, embodied; God in principle enters
the world. That is essentially no other than a continuation of the
meeting of God and world in the incarnation. This body of
Christ which is really present in the eucharistic symbol, is the
body of the Kyrios, Christ, exalted and transfigured by death and
resurrection.

When Ephesians 4 speaks of him who descended and ascended
once again in order to fill all things, this perspective of redemp-

---

[6] V. Warnach, "Kirche und Kosmos," in *Enkainia*, edited by H. Em-
onds, O.S.B. (Düsseldorf, 1956), p. 193.

tive history may probably also be found represented in the eucharist. The *katabasis* takes place for the sake of the *anabasis*. The entry of the divine into the mundane in the incarnation and the sacramental liturgical symbol, takes place in order to recover and bring back the world (not only the world of man but the entire creation, including the non-human creation) into the realm of God so that Christ may "fill all things". This ascent, this recovery, is perceptible in the sacrificed body of Christ, the "body of flesh" with which he has reconciled us by his death (Col. 1, 22). And so in the eucharistic sacrament the union of the divine and cosmic occurs. What is earthly is thus brought by the mystery of Christ into Christ's new plenitude of reality, and through the service of the Church it is drawn into the domain of the redemption. We must of course remember the merely provisional character of all symbols; no symbol can anticipate the perfect fulfillment or was meant to replace it. The sacramental symbol as such serves rather to open out the eschatological perspectives contained in the idea of the body of Christ in harmony with the movement of necessary growth and building up described in Ephesians 4, and which perpetually direct the body toward Christ its head. The body of Christ, the Church, grows toward its head by coming to a deeper realization and practice of what it is: the body of its Lord, and by constantly doing what Christ did for us: loving service.[7]

Christ's diaconia on the cross is the source of the Church. Since the Church is the body of Christ and constantly makes this an actual reality through the eucharistic body, the Church, too, is subject to the precept of diaconia and love of Christ. In this way the Church even now by way of sacramental sign incorporates the cosmic realms with itself in this process of growth toward the head. Since the body builds itself up by love—and does so sacramentally—it is obliged to loving service of the various domains of this world, so that they, too, may enter into the fullness of Christ. By taking the material, mundane sign of the sacrament into his service, and thus serving the world, Christ

[7] *Op. cit.*, pp. 200-5.

restores the cosmic realms to their own proper order. And that was also done as an example to the Church. Its relation to world, cosmos, universe is less a matter of rule or domination than of service. Certainly there is such a thing as the "world" in the Johannine sense, which is of the evil one and therefore must be overcome. And similarly the epistles of the captivity speak of the "powers" which must be subjugated. Nevertheless, it has to be noted that the overcoming of the world by Christ was accomplished by his great humiliation in the diaconia of the cross, and that this is the road which in principle is prescribed for the Church. It pursues it by the diaconia of the word and by loving fraternal service in the Christian community. But all this of course takes place exclusively in the human domain and within the Church. More consideration needs to be given to whether greater account should be taken of this in dealing with the most varied domains of what is generally called "the world". It would seem that under the heading of diaconia, new possibilities are opening out for that seriously compromised domain where Church and world meet.

The real sacrificial body of Christ becomes sacramentally present in the eucharist and unites the many who eat the bread into one body. This one body is a body "in Christ" or "body of Christ". It stands within Christ's sphere of influence and builds itself up in love. As the "body of Christ" it is mankind, united in the Church. Christ, the head of the body, has reconciled divided humanity and on the cross has brought it together into unity. He gives the body powers of growth. This body of Christ has cosmic perspectives. It brings the cosmic realms into the process of unification and recapitulation in Christ, until God is "all in all". The point at which this is already taking place even now, is the eucharist.

PART II
BIBLIOGRAPHICAL SURVEY

Heinz Schürmann/*Erfurt, West Germany*

Jesus' Words in the Light of His Actions at the Last Supper

The New Testament narratives of the institution of the last supper [1] consist of Lk. 22, 19-20 and the closely related 1 Cor. 11, 23b-25 from the same tradition, and, from another tradition, Mk. 14, 22-24 and, dependent on it, Mt. 26, 26-28 (with echoes also in Jn. 6, 51c, 53-56). In each case they report an action by Jesus in regard to the bread and wine cup and, in the course of this, in addition to various phrases of invitation, they report words which accompanied the two actions. These purport to interpret the actions by explaining Jesus' gift, the bread distributed and the proffered cup, or rather its content.

The accounts of Jesus' two actions in all four forms of the tradition are in fact relatively uniform, but the words that accompany them differ considerably. The differences clearly show that we do not know the actual words spoken by Jesus, and we can scarcely hope now to be able to reconstruct their original form behind these different versions. [2] We can hope with greater

---

[1] Details in H. Schürmann, article "Einsetzungsberichte," in *LThK* III (²1959), cols. 762-5 (most important literature here and in the cross-references). On Luke cf. *idem* "Lk. 22, 19a-20 als ursprüngliche Textüberlieferung," in *Biblica* 32 (1951) 364-92, 522-41.

[2] Cf. most recently the certainly much too skeptical investigation of F. Hahn, "Die alttestamentlichen Motive in der urchristlichen Abendmahlsüberlieferung," in *Evang. Theol.* 27 (1967), 337-74.

confidence to make out what Jesus actually did at the last supper. While it is of course the case that Jesus' action at the supper only becomes meaningful by what Jesus said, the facts of the history of traditions as we have stated them suggest that an attempt might be made to reach some firm basis for understanding Jesus' words at the last supper which have been handed down in different forms, by examining Jesus' actions at the last supper. This method has not really ever been consistently followed so far.[3]

I

The Double Eucharistic Action in the Lord's Supper of the Primitive Christians

1. What Took Place?

It is undisputed that in apostolic times and long after, the double eucharistic action with the bread and the cup was normally combined with an ordinary meal.

(a) The usual practice would be to place the eucharist after the ordinary meal [4] (cf. 1 Cor. 11, 17-26, especially v. 21 and elsewhere [5]). According to the custom of antiquity, the actual dinner was followed by a drinking session which as symposion, mishtītā, gave the whole banquet its name.[6] The early congregations will have given their fraternal suppers a festive character

---

[3] Since the paschal character of Jesus' last meal cannot be established with historical certainty either as a ritual paschal meal or as an anticipated and then modified paschal meal, for the New Testament sources only permit with certainty the conclusion that Jesus' last meal was a festal meal, it seems advisable in what follows to avoid argument on that basis. Cf. the article of Dequeker and Zuidema above.

[4] Cf. the demonstration in H. Schürmann, "Die Gestalt der urchristlichen Eucharistiefeier," in *Münch. Theol. Zeitschr.* 6 (1955), especially 117-22. The first evidence for the separation is found in the well-known letter of Pliny to Trajan (10, 96), perhaps also in Ignatius of Antioch, *ad Smyrn.* 8, and in Lk. 22, 19a (D it^{aur} sy^v), and then clearly in Justin, *Apol.* I, 65, 67.

[5] Cf. the form of meal described in Luke 22, 14-20ff.; Mark 14, 18-26a par Matthew, and probably also Acts 2, 42; 19, 7, 11; Col. 3, 12-17; Eph. 5, 15-20 and *Didaché* 9, 1-10, 6.

[6] Cf. G. Dalman, *Jesus-Jeschua* (Leipzig, 1922), 134.

(perhaps at first on the Lord's day) by following them with the eucharist in place of the drinking session, which was dropped. This arrangement would readily suggest itself because at Jewish banquets the drinking session was opened with the prayer of thanksgiving by the father of the family over the third cup of wine. There is no doubt that, as regards form history and history of tradition, the primitive Christian eucharistic prayer has its roots in this Jewish thanksgiving prayer.[7]

(b) This double action added to a meal, a eucharistic prayer spoken over bread and wine cup, then the distribution of bread and cup is certainly strangely unparalleled in the Hellenistic world. Its origin sets problems. It is, however, an almost universally accepted finding of research on the last supper [8] that here two meal rites have been juxtaposed; in origin these were a Jewish custom, the ritual beginning and end of a meal.[9] The stereotype phrase "after supper" handed down by Luke 22, 20 par 1 Corinthians 11, 25 plainly points to this. It was a characteristically Palestinian custom to "break bread" at the beginning of a meal.[10] In detail this involved "taking" into the hands the flat loaf of bread, the "breaking" with the eulogy, to which all answered "Amen", the "breaking" (or, better, "tearing") of the bread, the "giving," i.e., distribution of the bread.[11] This action has moved to the thanksgiving over the wine cup at the end of

[7] *Ibid.*, 134-44; H. L. Strack-P. Billerbeck, *Kommentar zum Neuen Testament aus Talmud und Midrash* (Munich, ³1956), 627-39, and also the bibliography in L. Ligier, "De la cène de Jésus à l'anaphore de l'église," in *Maison-Dieu* 87 (1966), 7-51.

[8] Especially now that the kiddush theory can be regarded as obsolete; cf. J. Jeremias, *Die Abendmahlsworte Jesu* (Göttingen, ⁴1966), 20-3; E. T. *The Eucharistic Words of Jesus*, 1966; and H. Lessig, *Die Abendmahlsprobleme im lichte der neutestamentlichen Forschung seit 1900*, (Diss. photom.), Bonn, 1953, 148ff. In 1 QS 6, 1-6 we should also think of the blessing of the bread as coming at the beginning of the meal and the blessing of the cup at the end; cf. Kuhn.

[9] Cf. H. Schürmann, "Die Gestalt der ursprünglichen Eucharistiefeier," 116f.

[10] "In non-Palestinian eyes something quite special," according to Lessig, *op. cit.* 270.

[11] Cf. Dalman, 122-8; Billerbeck, IV, 621-25; J. Geweib, Article "Brotbrechen," in *LThK* IV (²1958), col. 706f.

the meal. At a Jewish banquet the person presiding took a cup of wine (the third in the course of the meal) into his right hand, held it a hand's breadth over the table and pronounced over it the thanksgiving prayer to which all replied "Amen".[12] In the primitive Christian celebration of the eucharist (and at Jesus' last supper; see below), the wine cup of the father of the house was presented to all at table (Lk. 22, 17; Mk. 14, 23 par Mt.). By the process of fusion, a separate eulogy over the bread seems very early to have fallen into disuse, and the "eucharist" over the cup was also pronounced over the bread, thus combining the two original ceremonies into one double action. The combination of a rite for opening and a rite for closing a meal into a double action of this kind can only be explained by the fact that these ceremonies, which as Jewish customs were already strongly stylized, quasi-ritual gestures, were felt to be particularly full of meaning and also as belonging together. Why this was so, we must inquire. But to push the question further back, the origin of a double eucharistic action cannot be explained in terms of the life of the Hellenistic community.[13] Nor is it accounted for by Palestinian custom. Precisely for this reason everything supports the conclusion that here Jesus' actual actions had been coordinated and continued to be imitated. Furthermore, the indications point to a festive meal, since at least the action with the cup was not a feature of everyday meals. Now tradition tells us, and quite credibly, that it was the circumstances of Jesus' last supper which made it a solemn "farewell meal".[14]

[12] Cf. Schürmann, "Die Gestalt. . . ," 110f.
[13] We cannot distinguish, like H. Lietzmann, *Messe und Herrenmahl* (Bonn, 1926), 249-55, between a Jerusalem and a Pauline (cf. E. Lohmeyer, *Theol. Rundschau* 9 [1937], 273ff., and elsewhere: "Galilaean") type of Christian celebration of the Lord's supper (cf. also the thesis of a double origin in R. H. Fuller, *Biblical Research* 8 [1963], 1-15). At all events precisely these actions of the "Pauline type" are of characteristically Palestinian origin, cf. summary in Lessig, *op. cit.* 72-159. This alone is an objection to the theory of W. Marxsen, *Das Abendmahl als christologisches Problem* (Gütersloh, 1963), who regards its origin and meaning to consist solely in fellowship at table with Jesus.
[14] H. Schürmann, *Jesu Abschiedsnede Lk. 22, 21-38* (Ntl. Abh. XX/5), Münster, 1957, note 1.

2. Consequences for the History of the Tradition of the Institution Narratives

The above analysis of the origin of the eucharistic double action involves consequences for the historical understanding of the New Testament account of the institution of the eucharist. This account was probably not originally handed down in isolation, but represents an additional narrative added to complete the old "account of the paschal meal" (Lk. 22, 15-18=Mk. 14, 25 par Mt.).[15] The last supper logia reported in it (Luke 22, 16, 20=Mk. 14, 25 par Mt.) cannot, however, be played off [16] against the interpretative words of the accounts of institution. Moreover, the death prophecy of Luke 22, 18—in its original form [17]—does not explain the presentation of the cup and, above all, Luke 22, 16 does not explain why in addition to the action with the cup there is the "breaking of bread". The double action practiced in the Christian community cannot be understood from the account given in Luke 22, 15-18; its explanation is only to be found in the appended narrative of institution.

(a) The references to the setting in the narratives of institution therefore testify to Palestinian custom and point to a Palestinian origin for the Aramaic source which must be postulated behind the various traditions. Scholars are, however, largely in agreement that the Lucan-Pauline version of the institution narratives, at least in the references to the setting, is older than the Marcan (and Matthean) tradition, from which the archaic note "after supper" has disappeared and in which parallelism has been emphasized.[18]

(b) The realization that in the eucharistic double action two meal ceremonies originally divided by an actual meal have been

[15] Cf. H. Schürmann, Der Einsetzungsbericht Lk. 22, 19-20 (Ntl. Aph. XX/4), Münster, 1955, 133-50.

[16] Against the contention of E. Schweizer, Religion in Geschichte und Gegenwart, I (³1957), 15ff., of F. Hahn, Evang. Theol. 27 (1967), 340, 346, 368, and others.

[17] Cf. H. Schürmann, Der Paschamahlbericht Lk. 22, (7-14) 15-18 (Ntl. Aph. XIX/5), Münster, 1953, 53-73.

[18] Cf. H. Schürmann, Der Einsetzungsbericht, 83-93.

combined, also permits us to draw conclusions regarding the original form of the words spoken at the last supper which tradition has transmitted. Their chronological separation implies that each of the logia accompanying the actions must have had a form which was intelligible in itself—as in the parallelism, rising to a climax, of Luke 22, 19-20 par 1 Corinthians 11, 23-25. The logion over the bread cannot have been part of a synthetic parallelism intelligible solely on the basis of the logion over the wine which was spoken much later. This, however, is the case in Mark 14, 22-24 par Matthew. Here the two explanatory statements are closely coordinated and more closely assimilated ("body"— "blood") than in the asymmetrical Lucan-Pauline version ("body [given] for you"—"the new diatheke").[19] But although the asymmetrical version is probably closer to the original because the two rites were separated in time at the last supper (as well as for reasons drawn from the history of traditions), within the Lucan-Pauline tradition itself, the supplying of the copula in the wine logion and the second repetition in Paul's text of the command to repeat the action must be regarded as secondary.[20] The Lucan narrative of the institution must therefore be considered to be an independent [21] and at least in part older variant of the tradition which is also attested by Paul and which the latter had "received" as early as the year 40 in Antioch.

An analysis of the eucharistic double action therefore makes it

[19] Cf. *ibid.*, 107ff.

[20] Cf. *ibid.*, 30-4, 36-9. The prepositional expression with the article in the words over the bread in Paul ("which for you") is not as such possible in Aramaic, but it is very Pauline (cf. *ibid.* 17-30). Similarly the stressing of the pronouns is a Pauline modification (*ibid.*, 39ff, 60ff.). This contradicts the monotonously repeated postulate of P. Neuenzeit, *Das Herrenmahl* (Studien z.A.u.N.T. 1), Munich, 1960, that Paul must have handed on his tradition word for word.

[21] Cf. the demonstration in H. Schürmann, *Der Einsetzungsbericht*, 17-81. That is now also admitted by, among others, E. Schweizer, *Theol. Literat. Zeit.* 79 (1954), 577-592; Lessig, *op. cit.;* A. Oepke, *Theol. Literat. Zeit.* 80 (1955), 129-42; G. Bornkamm, *N. T. Stud.* 2 (1955/56), 202-6; *idem, Zeitschr. f. Theol. u.* Kirche 53 (1956), 312-449; Hahn, *op. cit.,* 339. P. Benoit is still critical, "The Eucharistic Narratives of Institution and Their Significance" (1956), in *Exégèse et Dogmatique.*

possible for us to examine the various traditions of the institution narratives and last supper logia with a view to establishing which is closest to the original.

II
JESUS' ACTIONS AT THE LAST SUPPER

The primitive Christian "Lord's supper" (1 Cor. 11, 20) is not to be regarded simply as a repetition of Jesus' last supper, for this, as a farewell meal, could not be repeated. It was the daily meals of the original community (cf. Acts 2, 42-46) which represented a continuation of Jesus' day to day life with his disciples. The eucharistic double action at the end of the primitive Christian "Lord's supper", on the other hand, as we have just seen from the history of tradition, had its origin in actions performed by Jesus on the occasion of his last supper: [22] in the "breaking of bread" which opened the meal and the "eucharist" over the cup which closed it,[23] two rites which after Easter were brought together and imitated because of their significance.

What did their significance consist in? Certainly not merely in the commands to repeat them as asserted in Luke 22, 19—1 Corinthians 11, 24f. In appearance, Jesus had merely taken up two rites already customary at Jewish meals. A key to understanding is provided if we attend—this has scarcely ever been done systematically—to the two departures from what was customary in what Jesus did.

1. Parallel to the distribution of the bread, Jesus, contrary to usual custom,[24] as cannot be sufficiently stressed, gave his cup to all those at table to drink.

[22] This indicates the element of truth in the thesis of Lietzmann (see note 13 above).

[23] Catholic authors who recognize the chronological separation of Jesus' two actions at the last supper are listed in *Biblica* 32 (1951), 534, note 2; see also Benoit, *op. cit.*

[24] Cf. H. Schürmann, *Der Paschamahlbericht,* 60f., against Dalman, *op. cit.* 140f., and the majority.

2. As the institution narratives show, Jesus is said to have added some words of explanation when he distributed the bread and the cup. That is quite likely,[25] because only in that way could the significance which, as we have noted was attributed to the two fundamental meal ceremonies, be made clear. These two special features go together, explain and support one another.

1. *The Meaning of Jesus' Double Action*

(a) The distribution of the bread broken at the beginning of a Jewish meal did not bear the meaning of giving those present a share in the prayer [26]—this was done by the "Amen". The prayer was rather felt to be in some way a blessing,[27] and consequently the piece of bread symbolically presented was felt to be salutary. That is suggested by many Jewish sources according to which food and drink are divine gifts.[28] The distribution gave the master of the house an opportunity to put his "beautiful eye", i.e., his benevolent attitude, into the sharing out.[29] This interpretation of the distribution of the bread is supported by the meaning of the parallel distribution of the cup.

(b) When, contrary to the usual custom, perhaps for that very reason with an express command (Lk. 22, 17; cf. Mt. 2, 25) Jesus gave his cup to all at table to drink (Lk. 22, 17; Mk. 14, 23 par Mt.), he was probably resuming a not unusual Jewish custom. The father of the house could "send" his cup to a guest at the meal who was to be specially honored or to a member of the family in another room who was not taking part in the meal; this later became the general custom with the consecrated cup on sabbaths and festivals.[30] That, however, expressed a very special

[25] Contrary to the skepticism of Lessig, *op. cit.* 274-81.
[26] This is frequently repeated after G. Dalman, 125f., 140f.
[27] Cf. H. Schürmann, *Der Paschamahlbericht,* 62f. W. Schrenk, *Der Segen im Neuen Testament* (Berlin, 1967), 125-30, does not see how the new eucharistic content modifies the language and makes possible the use of *eulogein* with an object in the accusative (1 Cor. 10, 16; cf. Mk. 8, 7; Lk. 9, 16).
[28] Cf. J. Jeremias, *Die Abendmahlsworte Jesu,* 225-8.
[29] According to *b. Ber.* 46a; cf. Dalman, *Jesus-Jeschua,* 126.
[30] Cf. *ibid.,* 140.

good wish, from which all kinds of salutary effects might be expected.[31] Jesus' general distribution of the cup was therefore striking in itself; and at his hands it was something very special. Consequently, the distribution of the bread and cup suggests the interpretation that Jesus intended—we must be careful of our expression for the moment—to signify or convey a blessing.

2. Consequences for the Tradition of the Lord's Words

If we have succeeded in showing that it is probable that the breaking of bread and the proffering of the cup, as Jesus' own actions—*ipsissima facta*—are two significant gestures of donation, then the words which specify the gift are almost inescapably postulated as Jesus' own actual words—*ipsissima verba*—even apart from the question whether we can historically deduce them word for word.

The four traditions agree that in the words which accompanied the distribution Jesus specified the proffered gift and did so in two respects. With the wine cup he gave a share in a (new) covenant; this covenant, however, is brought into connection with his imminent death, which is referred to not only in the logion over the cup but also in the logion of the bread in all the versions of the tradition. With the help of various Old Testament themes, strong theological forces were certainly operative in the words at the last supper. Although the reconstruction of an original form is no longer possible, perhaps some idea can be formed of it.

(a) If Jesus' distribution of bread and cup pointed significantly to a blessing bestowed, we would be chiefly inclined to think of the gift of eschatological salvation, for, after all, this was the focus of all Jesus' preaching (cf. simply Mk. 1, 14f.). Furthermore, Jesus had often represented this under the image of a banquet.[32] Now our oldest account of the last supper (Lk. 22,

---

[31] Cf. the texts quoted by Dalman, *ibid.*, 140, restricted and supplemented by Billerbeck IV, 59, 60 Comparison should be made with statements such as Pss. 16, 4f.; 116, 13. Further details in H. Schürmann, *Der Paschamahlbericht*, 60-5.

[32] Examples in the authors listed by Lessig, *op. cit.* note 445.

15-18 par Mark 14, 25) also opens out a perspective full of hope beyond the double prophecy of death on the eschatological world of God.[33] A similar hope is given in the promise of Luke 22, 28ff., which must have been linked very early with the institution narrative of Luke 22, 15-18.[34]

The promised eschatological "new covenant" of Jer. 31, 31-34 is therefore probably also meant by the cup logion of Luke and Paul (if we are not also to remember Is. 42, 6; 49, 8), and by the logion over the wine in Mark (and Matthew)—superseding in fact the Sinai covenant in Exodus 24, 8 (cf. the heavenly covenant banquet in Ex. 24, 9-11). The idea of the covenant in Jeremiah 31, 31-34 in the eschatological form of the Lucan-Pauline version, however, must be closer to the original than the cultic reminder of Exodus 24, 8 in the wine logion of Mark (and Matthew).[35]

(b) The circumstances of the farewell meal make it natural to suppose that in Jesus' distribution of bread and wine cup, emphasized by accompanying words, there is a reference to his imminent death. The attempt has repeatedly been made to understand Jesus' double action at the last supper in some "symbolic" way [36] and to find in it an allusion to his death. But none can be found in the "separation of the sacramental species", nor in the everyday action of breaking the bread or of pouring out the wine (which does not in fact take place), nor in the broken bread and the red color of the wine (which is not mentioned). At most it may be seen in the distribution of a nourishing food and a comforting drink.[37] We must reckon with the possibility that the distribution of a "salvific gift" at a meal which was celebrated precisely as a farewell meal was meant to give a farewell gift, bestow the blessing of the imminent death and thereby

[33] Lessig, *ibid.*, 308, observes "that there is general agreement about the presence of a reference to the eschatological expectation in Jesus' last supper". Cf. on this theme, P. Lebeau, *Le vin nouveau du royaume* (Museum Lessianum, sect. bibl. 5), Paris-Brussels, 1966.

[34] Cf. H. Schürmann, *Jesu Abschiedsrede Lk. 22, 21-38*, 99-116.

[35] Cf. H. Schürmann, *Der Einsetzungsbericht*, 110f.

[36] Cf. the various symbolical interpretations listed in Lessig, 308-13.

[37] Cf. the authors named by Lessig, *op. cit.* notes 1095 and 1105.

at the same time illumine the meaning of that death. The presumption of the eschatological meaning of Jesus' gift at such an hour should not obscure the thought of death; the irruption of the eschaton must be thought of in conjunction with Jesus' death. In fact the ancient paschal meal narrative of Luke 14, 16, 18 shows Jesus pronouncing as his last words a double prophecy of death (not a "vow of renunciation" [38]), in an eschatological perspective, so that the proffered gift of blessing can also, in harmony with this old tradition, be brought into connection with the imminent death. And the words at the last supper that have been handed down to us, for all their differences, also agree in affirming that Jesus brought the proffered bread into relation with his (Lk.: "given") "body" (Lk. and 1 Cor. 11: "for you"), and the proffered cup into relation with his death (= "blood"). And the death is unanimously understood as a redemptive death (Lk. and 1 Cor. 11: "for you"; Mk. and Mt.: "for many") and all four accounts regard it as constituting a covenant.

Despite these common elements, the words of explanation in Luke (and Paul) on the one hand, and of Mark (and Matthew) on the other, express very different theologoumena. In Luke (not so strictly in Paul), Jesus' death is understood as the vicarious expiatory death of the *Ebed Yahweh* (Is. 53); in Mark (and Matthew) on the other hand, it is seen in the light of the cultic sacrifice of Exodus 24, 8. Perhaps we may regard the Lucan-Pauline interpretation of Jesus' death in the light of Isaiah 53 as closer to the original than the cultic sacrificial conception of Mark (and Matthew), especially as the application of the idea of sacrifice to the death of a man must have been alien to Palestinian Judaism.[39]

The logion of the bread with its attributive addition in Luke ("which is given for you"), like his wine logion should be understood in the light of Isaiah 53.[40] In Mark (and Matthew), on the other hand, "body" and "blood" are viewed together sym-

[88] Contrary to J. Jeremias' view, cf. H. Schürmann, *Der Paschamahl-bericht*, 53-73.
[89] Cf. H. Schürmann, *Der Einsetzungsbericht*, 95-112.
[40] Cf. *ibid.*, 115-123.

metrically in accordance with the idea of a cultic sacrifice; if originally Jesus' two actions at the last supper were separated in time, however, this synthesis cannot be the original.

For all their differences, the words of the last supper unanimously declare that a share in the atoning powers of Jesus' (sacrificial) death and the gifts of the new covenant, is given to anyone who allows himself to be given the proffered bread and wine cup as saving food and saving drink.

In retrospect a probable interpretation would seem to be that at his farewell meal, Jesus turned the usual "breaking of bread" at the beginning of the meal and the customary offering of the cup at its end into a symbolic action anticipating his imminent death, an ôt rather in the manner of the Old Testament prophets.[41] But here it is not really a case of prophesying the future; prophesied future is proffered as a gift. John the Baptist by pouring water had already symbolically and effectively acted out the prophecy, "I will sprinkle clean water upon you, and you shall be clean . . ." (Ezek. 36, 25; cf. Zech. 13, 1). Similarly, on this view, by his double action at the last supper, Jesus would have effectively proffered eschatological salvation as the fruit of his death, and by doing so also represented it symbolically.[42] The Baptist's salvific action and that of Jesus presuppose the prophecy, take it up, make it a reality and apply it, and are therefore more than a prophetic ôt.[43] It should be noted that compared with the Greek conception of the sacraments, the direction of the symbolism is reversed. The pouring of the water by the Baptist and Jesus' distribution of bread and wine, signify something by doing and giving something.[44] The sign is in the gift, the gift is

[41] Cf. G. Fohrer, *Die symbolischen Handlungen der Propheten* (Abh. z. Theol. A.u.N.T. 25), Zurich, 1953.

[42] Authors who take this view, but with various interpretations, are listed by Lessig, note 1112; cf. also the following note.

[43] Contrary to the view of J. Dupont, "Ceci est mon corps"; "Ceci est mon sang," in *Nouv. Rev. Théol.* 80 (1958), 1025-41, and J. Betz, *Die Eucharistie in der Zeit der griechischen Väter* I/1, Freiburg-Basel-Vienna 1961, especially 46-59.

[44] Kuhn admits that the actions attested in the narratives of institution must be declared to be the *ipsissima facta* of Jesus, but thinks that what

not the effect of the sign. The effected gift signifies something, the sign does not primarily effect something. The disclosure of such symbolism does not exclude a realistic conception of the eucharist; on the contrary, it presupposes it.[45] The words which accompany the distribution are intended to signify and set forth predicatively what kind of a saving food is actually being given with the bread and the wine cup which in so unusual a way is distributed to all. Bread and cup are certainly not distributed as food and drink in order to represent Jesus' death as salvific purely symbolically (*sacramentum tantum*), but because they are salvific gifts. And the explanatory words are not merely intended to identify what is proffered with "body" and "blood" (*sacramentum et res*) but, in different ways, are emphatically concerned to characterize them as saving gift (*res sacramenti*).

---

was originally a symbolic action on Jesus' part was subsequently "sacramentalized" in the Hellenistic communities. But the interpretation we suggest makes it unnecessary to assume this.

[45] Cf. the detailed treatment in the two works referred to in note 43 above.

Herman Schmidt, S. J. / *Rome, Italy*

Transformation of the Roman Celebration of the Eucharist

The history of the liturgy shows that radical changes in the culture of the West have exerted such a strong influence on the forms of worship and in particular on the celebration of the eucharist that it is legitimate to employ the word *transformation*. Not only were the existing structures modified by incidental alterations, adaptations, innovations, retouchings, improvements, extensions or simplifications, but the whole celebration underwent an internal metamorphosis, reshaping or remodelling.[1] The liturgy is essentially so deeply rooted in the various cultures that it necessarily follows the fluctuations in the changing stream of human existence. The very words *cultura* and *cultus,* which both come from the same root, *colere* (cultivate, tend), already point in this direction. But the fundamental reason for this phenomenon lies, so far as Chris-

[1] A detailed bibliography of liturgical history is given by (among others), H. Schmidt, *Introductio in liturgiam occidentalem* (Rome, Herder, ³1966), p. 202 (studies of A. Mayer), 413ff. (Eucharist), 742-47 (general). A selection is to be found in *Bibliographia ad usum seminariorum* (Nijmegen: Bestel Centrale V.S.K.B., English version 1961, French 1960, German 1959), Vol. 1. The most recent history of the so-called eucharistic devotion was written by A. van Bruggen, *Réflexion sur l'adoration eucharistique* (Rome: Libreria Francese, 1968). A short but well-informed survey is provided by W. Godel, *Die Entwicklung des römischen Kultverständnisses vom Frühmittelalter bis zum II. Vatikanischen Konzil* in *Kult und Kontemplation in Ost und West* (Regensburg: Pustet, 1967), pp. 110-40.

tian worship is concerned, in the true incarnation of the divine Word: nothing human is alien to the Church of Christ any more than it is to Christ himself. The liturgy is and remains really divine, *divinum officium,* if at the same time it is at all times and in all places truly and fully human.

After the Council of Trent when the official liturgy came to stand outside the cultural development of humanity, violence was done to it. Because nature is stronger than doctrine the result was that around the sacred enclosure of the liturgy there arose pseudo- or para-liturgies in which the people could express its religious feelings. Even today it is well known with what kind of devotional exercises people used to keep themselves piously occupied during Mass.[2]

With the promulgation of the *Constitution on the Sacred Liturgy* (December 4, 1963) Vatican Council II gave the modern, living languages a place to worship. Few suspected on December 4, 1963 that this decision would bring enormous consequences with it. It is true that the Council ordered a serious review of the liturgical texts, but now that the preliminaries are over the execution of this order looks so complicated that the greatest prudence is required if the result is not to be a disillusionment. More and more voices can be heard expressing seriously founded concern; and indications of this concern can be traced back to the first general gathering of the synod of bishops, which met from September 29 to October 29, 1967.

In brief, the problems involved are the following:

1. The introduction of living languages requires a thorough knowledge of the contemporary sciences of language and translation. The *Societas Liturgica,* an ecumenical learned society for the study of the liturgy founded at Driebergen on July 26-30, 1967, is organizing an international congress on language and

---

[2] *Pia* or *sacra exercitia* arose as early as the Romanesque and Gothic periods and threatened then to stifle the Latin liturgy. The fact that after the Council of Trent a sharp line was drawn between the old liturgy and the new devotions produced the result that the Roman liturgy has come down to us as a venerable cultural monument of the first millennium of the Christian era.

liturgy which is to take place at the beginning of September, 1969.[3]

2. Between the Roman liturgy and contemporary cultures lies a gap of centuries, since in the Roman Catholic Church the peoples and nations possess no liturgical traditions of their own. Now that the Roman liturgy lies open to inspection in the living languages it begins to look archaic and seems not to function as it should. A return to the original form of the Roman liturgy would be to indulge in archaeology. The adaptation and retouching of old texts and ceremonies must frequently fail because of the risk of mutilating the liturgical inheritance without really achieving the radical changes demanded by the men of today. A contemporary liturgical culture must be developed everywhere, and this demands time for responsible experimentation. Article 23 of the *Constitution on the Sacred Liturgy,* which speaks of holding on to tradition while permitting legitimate development, is cautious in tone but not frightened of innovation: let the path be opened to legitimate development, it says (*via legitimae progressioni aperiatur*), but innovations should only be adopted if this is demanded by the true and certain interest of the Church (*innovationes ne fiant nisi vera et certa utilitas Ecclesiae id exigat*); the new forms must grow organically and out of the existing forms (*novae formae ex formis iam exstantibus quodammodo crescant*).

3. The development of knowledge (including theology in all its branches) has been so radical in the last century that if the liturgy wants to have something to say to the men of today it must follow this development and apply its results. What Pius XII said to liturgists on the occasion of the Congress at Assisi on September 22, 1956 still remains topical: "The liturgy of today is also continually occupied with numerous special problems such as the relationship of the liturgy to the religious ideas of the

---

[3] A report was issued on the congress held under the auspices of the "Consilium ad exsequendam Constitutionem de sacra liturgia": *Le traduzioni dei libri liturgica. Atti del congresso tenuto a Roma il 9-13 novembre 1965* (Vatican City, 1966). No further bibliographical information can be given here because the theme is too wide.

present-day world, to contemporary culture, social questions and depth psychology." [4] The conviction becomes steadily stronger that the contemporary transformation of the liturgy must be marked by openness to the humanity of the future in all its multiplicity and with all its problems. The old adage *sacramenta propter homines* and the still older "symbolum fidei" which says of Christ *"qui propter nos homines et propter nostram salutem descendit de caelis"* [5] apply to the forms of worship, too.

What has been succinctly outlined above with reference to the liturgy in general is clearly evident at its center, the Roman celebration of the eucharist. A series of decrees has given this celebration a new look. The eucharist, including the Roman canon,

[4] *A.A.S.* 48 (1956), p. 724.

[5] The following are details of some articles which have dared to take a critical attitude to the future of the liturgy: L. Bright, "The Liturgical Community," in *The Committed Church* (London: Darton, Longman and Todd, 1966), pp. 243-52; D. Callahan, "The Renewal Mess," in *Commonweal* 10 (1967), pp. 621-25; G. Diekmann, "The Reform of Catholic Liturgy. Are We Too Late?" in *Worship* 41 (1967), pp. 142-51; J. Macquarrie, "Subjectivity and Objectivity in Theology and Worship," in *Worship* 41 (1967), pp. 152-60; Th. Maertens, "Que deviennent le mouvement et la réforme liturgiques?" in *Rev. Nouv.* 15 (Nov. 1967); H. Manders, "Désacralisation de la liturgie," in *Paroisse et Liturgie* 48 (1966), pp. 702-17; H. Manders, "De liturgie en de mens," in *Tijdschr. Liturg.* 52 (1968), pp. 56-69; Fr. Roustang, "Le troisième homme," in *Christus* 52 (1966) pp. 561-67; E. Schillebeeckx. "Wereldlijke eredienst en kerkelijke liturgie," in *Tijdschr. Theol.* 7 (1967), pp. 288-302; H. Schmidt, "Le renouveau liturgique," in *Nouv. Rev. Theol.* 98 (1966), pp. 807-29; W. Snels, "Bidden in een profane wereld," in *Theol. en Pastoraat* 63 (1967), pp. 17-24; P. Vanbergen, "La crise de la liturgie," in *Paroisse et Liturgie* 49 (1967), pp. 463-71, 642-59, 739-63, and 50 (1968), pp. 157-60; F. Vandenbroucke, "Le point de vue du consommateur," in *Quest. Lit. Par.* 7 (1966), pp. 225-31; B. Wicker, "The Church: A Radical Concept of Community," in *The Committed Church* (London: Darton, Longman and Todd, 1966), pp. 253-79; "Wie steht es um die Liturgiereform?" in *Herder Korrespondenz* 22 (1968), pp. 83-8.
Contributions on the liturgy and human sciences appear in *La Maison-Dieu* 91 (1967) and 93 (1968), pp. 103-45; *Tijdschr. Lit.* 51 (1967), pp. 121-84 and 52 (1968), pp. 1-104; and *La liturgie après Vatican II* (Unam Sanctam, 66), Paris: Ed. du Cerf, 1967.
Contemporary problems are treated in these books: "Ist der Mensch von heute noch liturgiefähig?" *Liturgie und Mönchtum,* 38 (1966); G. Deussen, *Die neue liturgische Gemeinde* (Frankfurt: Knecht, 1968); R. Falsini-M. Morganti-A. Piacentini, "Perchè la la riforma liturgica?" in

is now celebrated in the vernacular, an innovation which brings with it profound changes in the musical interpretation. The rite has been simplified and made more flexible, primarily with a view to the active participation of the congregation in the proceedings. Three or four new canons have been or are being authorized alongside the Roman canon, and this signifies an unfamiliar element of variation. Because they are effective, these external alterations are also causing an internal transformation that goes deeper and is more radical and creative in its aims. What was once typically static is now suddenly becoming so dynamic that applying the brake is of little use and the planned development threatens to get out of hand. The traditional Roman structure of the eucharistic celebration is being called into question: mere restoration and adaptation are felt to be inadequate. With the assistance of comparative liturgical and religious studies, an attempt is being made, on the basis of Scripture and of apostolic and ecclesiastical tradition, to discover the fundamental structure of the eucharist and then to bring into being a more firmly based contemporary eucharistic celebration. In other words, now that for all practical purposes *Latin* is disappearing the *Roman* element is also being called into question.[6] Two important concrete points need to be elucidated somewhat further.

1. In the post-conciliar celebration of the eucharist the *liturgy of the Word of God* has regained its proper place next to, and in, the sacrament: the faithful are given a biblical orientation in their thinking and living. Next to the use of the vernacular the most important factors in this biblical revival are the new lec-

---

Quaderni di orientamenti pastorali 13 (Milan: Massimo, 1967). In connection with contemporary liturgical problems various publications of J. Jungmann are still topical.

[6] Some writers have worked out a plan for a so-called ecumenical Mass, which is intended to serve as the basic structure of all rites. The most detailed approach is to be found in Klaus Gamber, *Liturgie Uebermorgen. Gedanken über die Geschichte und Zukunft des Gottesdienstes* (Freiburg: Herder, 1966). The assembly of a basic structure was the point of departure of the so-called *Missa normativa* (Rahmenmesse) of the "Consilium ad exsequendam Constitutionem de sacra liturgia"; as is known, it provoked a lively discussion with unavoidable confusion because of the originality of the plan.

tionaries with pericopes covering several years and a rite aiming at a true proclamation, including the element of resonance of the Word in the hearts of the faithful (acclamations and singing). The Old Roman proclamation-structure has now become clear: Old Testament reading—gradual—reading from an apostle—tract or alleluia-verse—Gospel—homily—prayer of the faithful.

But the place accorded to Scripture has at the same time aroused criticism. The efforts of liturgists to make three readings obligatory on Sundays and feast days provokes a reaction from the clergy: no obligation, they say, but freedom of choice in the number of readings (three, two or even one). They would also like to treat the lectionary system as a guideline, not as a strict obligation. The Bible as a whole, they point out, is the finest liturgical book, which should normally be read and expounded according to the original method, the so-called *lectio continua;* the liturgical "game" (a word gladly used by liturgists) of combining two or three readings on the same theme from different books sometimes has surprising results but often seems forced. Furthermore, the old Roman proclamation-structure is felt to be archaic, especially by younger men. It may well have been valid, they say, in an age of illiteracy, but is no longer so in an age of reading, illustrations and mass-media techniques (films, film strips, shows, radio, television.[7]

At the same time the breviary and the celebration of the Word of God [8] are rightly drawn into the discussion because they are centered on the eucharist. In the breviary (which for 90% of the clergy is bound to be a "reading" book and not a by-product of "choir" prayer) and in the celebration of the Word there is a need for biblical commentaries, including commentaries on the psalms, which are not just borrowed from the Fathers but newly put together from the vast store of recent exegesis and biblical theology. As a result, people are beginning to see the importance, in the proclamation of the Word, of dialogue, so many

[7] It is worth making acquaintance with the main chapter, "Liturgies de masse," in E. Gilson, *La société de masse et sa culture* (Essais d'art et de philosophie, Paris: Vrin, 1967), pp. 107-9.

[8] Cf. n. 35 of the *Constitution on the Sacred Liturgy.*

examples of which are familiar from the life of Christ; a new form of spirituality is growing up in the shape of Bible clubs and discussion groups, where a joint effort is made to discover God's purposes and plans by looking in the Bible and at current events. What is the point, people finally ask, in first reading extracts which a simple congregation does not understand and then explaining or adapting parts of them in the homily? Reading and explanation should in many cases be combined, though without distorting the objectivity of God's Word by subjective interpretations.[9]

The transformation of the liturgy of the Word is inspired by what can be read in Vatican Council II's *Constitution on Divine Revelation:* the divine Scriptures "impart the Word of God himself without change, and make the voice of the Holy Spirit resound in the words of the prophets and apostles"; "in the sacred books, the Father who is in heaven meets his children with great love and speaks with them"; "prayer should accompany the reading of sacred Scripture, so that God and man may talk together" (nn. 21 and 25). In the liturgy of today efforts are being made to establish a genuine conversation between God and contemporary man without holding fast *a priori* to structures and forms which though worthy of the greatest respect must also in all honesty be regarded as transitory.

2. The problems of the Mass are becoming more serious in the sphere of the *sacramental action.* The translation of the Roman canon and the introduction of new canons undoubtedly involve the people more closely in what the Instruction, *Euchar-isticum mysterium,* calls "the celebration of the memory of the Lord".[10] Yet, in practice, these alterations are not adequate, and for two reasons. First of all, the texts are felt to be a barrier or curtain between the people, frequently including the clergy, and Christ; as a result they remain a priestly monologue addressed to the congregation without effectively drawing it into the actual

---

[9] See J. Brynes, "Preaching; Present Possibilities and Perennial Value," in *Worship* 41 (1968), pp. 14-21.

[10] S. Congregatio Rituum, *Instructio de cultu mysterii eucharistici* (die 25 maii 1967), *A.A.S.* 59 (1967), p. 551.

proceedings. In other words, we have not yet arrived at what the old Roman liturgy fittingly called the *canon actionis,* that is, a "line of action", for the texts remain unshakable ritual formulas full of problems, obscurities and anachronisms. In consequence the assembled congregation is not led to take a fully active part in the dialogue and ceremonial actions. This brings the danger of a "talk" liturgy and, still worse, of "talking over people's heads". It would be foolish to suppose that serious liturgists are not aware of these problems; thoroughgoing plans are in existence, and on a high level, too, but one cannot break iron with one's bare hands, and obstinate ritualism presents just as much resistance.

Vagaggini has made serious criticisms of the Roman canon and himself put forward new suggestions, which likewise aroused criticism.[11] The translators of the Roman canon do not feel happy with the results of their work, again because of subsequent interventions by non-experts.[12] Since the new canons have not yet been tested in practice or discussed in the press no verdict can yet be passed on them in a bibliographical survey of this sort.

There also exist personal schemas for new canons, which merit attentive and objective study.[13] These are intended to be contemporary and therefore are successful in practice but encounter opposition from professional theologians and liturgists. These experts like to recall various *a priori* assumptions, in their view unshakable, which they miss in the new schemas. They also

[11] C. Vagaggini, *Il Canone della Messa e la riforma liturgica* (Quaderni di Rivista liturgica, 4) (Turin-Leumann, Elle di ci, 1966); J. Jungmann, "Um die Reform des römischen Kanons. Eine kritische Stellungnahme zu C. Vagagginis Entwürfen," in *Liturg. Jahrb.* 17 (1967), pp. 1-17.

[12] One can catch this dissatisfaction in various liturgical journals. R. Falsini is frank in *Riv. Past. Theol.* 6 (1968), pp. 131-51, and in *Il Canone della Messa* (Sussidi liturgico pastorali, 19) Milan, 1968, pp. 55-82. A more official discussion is to be found in *The Roman Canon in English Translation* (London: Chapman, 1968).

[13] See for example in *Paroisse et Liturgie* 49 (1967) pp. 219-59 and pp. 431-36; *Liturg. Jahrb.* 18 (1968), pp. 44-60; *Riv. Liturg.* 54 (1967), pp. 513-43.; C. Berti-I. Calabuig, *Due progetti di Canone eucaristico per il rito romano nella luce ecumenica* (Bibliotheca "Ephemerides Liturgicae" 31, Rome, 1967), and *Saggi di Canone eucaristico per le Messe delle ordinazione, nozze, esequie e degli infermi* (Scripta facultatis theologicae "Marianum" 21, Rome, 1968).

sometimes make a radical distinction between "vertical" and "horizontal" prayer, a distinction which to me among others seems forced and open to question, a sort of slogan with a pseudo-scientific tinge. In connection with the new schemas it is worth noting something which has already been pointed out earlier: they cut loose from the trusted models and go freely back to the original sources in Scripture and Tradition in order to find valid modes of expression for modern-day Churches. What this explanatory volume of *Concilium* provides is the basis and inspiration of the whole transformation of the eucharistic celebration.

So long as it really proceeds in spirit and truth the development is not be held back, in spite of opposition due to understandable anxiety or provisional incomprehension. The serious crisis in the Church compels us to take courageous and thorough measures even in the realm of the purely religious and solely Christian. Inspired by a speech of Paul VI,[14] Joannes wrote: "Only a community which has rediscovered tradition and lives intensively on it is in a position to 'bring forth' new forms or to understand and assimilate new conceptions. On the other hand, one cannot imagine that a Church which has been renewed in her consciousness of faith and in her inner piety could long be chained to clumsy liturgical formulas. Living man lives by expressing himself, and any suppression of this activity is bound to bring with it a depression of his *élan vital.*" [15]

[14] General audience August 9, 1967, *Oss. Rom.* Aug. 10, 1967.
[15] V. Joannes, "Quelques problèmes du renouveau liturgique," IDO-C doss. 67-35. See also: "Le Synode et le renouveau liturgique," IDO-C doss. 67-40.

PART III
DOCUMENTATION
CONCILIUM

Office of the Executive Secretary
Nijmegen, Netherlands

Concilium General Secretariat/*Nijmegen, Netherlands*
Ernst Ehrlich/*Basle, Switzerland*
Marc Tanenbaum/*New York, New York*

How Modern Jews Celebrate Their History

T he aforegoing articles must already have made it clear that the institution of the eucharist did not mean a total break with the worship of the people to whom Jesus belonged. Is this worship then a past glory which can only be a help toward a better understanding of the New Testament celebration of God's presence or is this worship still a living reality for the Jews of our own age? To obtain some genuine information about this problem we have put a few questions to Jewish experts, and these questions with the replies given constitute the contents of this documentation.[1] We are therefore not primarily concerned here with a historical description of Jewish feasts but principally with showing that Jewish worship is today still a living reality which cannot fail to be a cohesive element for the Jewish community. For the rest, Jewish worship has al-

[1] For suggestions and the replies to our questions we wish to express our gratitude to Rabbi Marc H. Tanenbaum, director of the interreligious affairs department of the American Jewish Committee of New York, Prof. Dr. J. Maier of the *Martin Buber Institute für Judiastik* at Cologne University, M. Zaoui of the *Institut International des Etudes Hébraïques* in Paris, the *Institute for Studies of Contemporary Judaism* at the Hebrew University of Jerusalem, Prof. Dr. M. Wittenberg of the Augustana-Hochschule of Neuendettelschau, Dr. Gertrud Luckner of the *Freiburger Rundbrief*, so important for the ecumenical relations between Christians and Jews, K. Hruby, and Dr. E. L. Ehrlich for his important contribution on Passah and Atonement, of which we have made extensive use in this documentation.

ways a certain appeal for Christians.[2] They have always seen there the roots from which their own worship developed.[3]

One difficulty in this documentation was the fact that Judaism today does not show such an absolute uniformity as some might think.[4] Modern Judaism shows a high degree of pluriformity in its worship. Moreover, this worship does not constitute for all Jews the same kind of bond that links them to the People of God. Modern Judaism has also begun to think historically and critically and puts the ethical reality at the heart of its worship so that the ritual element only plays a marginal role in the Jewish con-

[2] A few striking illustrations of the appeal Jewish worship has on Christians may be found in *Kirche und Synagoge, Handbuch zur Geschichte von Christen und Juden*, I (Stuttgart, 1968), pp. 495-8: G. Müller, "Die jüdische Gottesverehrung und ihre Anziehungskraft."

[3] Not much has been written recently on this subject; we refer to the basic volume of H. N. Rowley, *Worship in Ancient Israel. Its Forms and Meaning* (London, 1967); H. Tanenbaum, *The Jewish Holidays* (New York, n. d.); F. Weinreb, *The Old Biblical Year* (pro ms, Geneva, 1968); D. Baumgardt, "Yom Kippur and the Jew of Today," in *Commentary* (Oct. 1959); E. L. Ehrlich, *Kultsymbolik im Alten Testament und im nachbiblischen Judentum* (Stuttgart, 1959); W. Gottschalk, *Judentum. Schicksal, Wesen und Gegenwart* (Wiesbaden, 1965); Th. H. Gaster, *Passover* (London-New York, 1958); E. D. Goldschmidt, *Die Pesach-Haggada* (Berlin, 1937); J. Henninger, "Ueber Frühlingsfeste bei den Semiten," in *In Verbo Tuo* (1963); K. Hruby, "Le Yom Ha-Kippurim ou Jour de l'Expiation," in *L'Orient Syrien* 10, nn. 1, 2, 4 (1965); R. R. Geis, *Vom unbekannten Judentum* (Freiburg, 1961); G. G. Scholem, *Major Trends in Jewish Mysticism* (London, 1955, 3rd ed.); E. R. Goodenough, *Jewish Symbols in the Graeco-Roman Period* (New York, 1954); S. W. Baron, *Social and Religious History of the Jews* (Philadelphia, 1952); H. J. Kraus, *Gottesdienst in Israel* (Munich, 1962, 2nd ed.); H. Schauss, *Guide to Jewish Holidays* (New York, 1962); J. B. Segal, *The Hebrew Passover* (London, 1963); J. Soetendorp, *Symbolik der jüdischen Religion* (Gütersloh, 1963); S. Stein, "The Influence of Symposia Literature on the Literary Form of the Pesach Haggada," in *Journal of Jewish Studies* 8 (1957), pp. 13f.; the contributions by M. H. Tanenbaum and E. L. Ehrlich which have been used in this documentation have been supplemented with data about the Jewish feasts from the *Standard Jewish Encyclopedia* of C. Roth (London, 1962) and J. F. Oppenheimer, E. Ben Gurion and E. G. Lowenthal, *Lexikon des Judentums* (London, etc., 1967) and from R. de Vaux, *Les Institutions de l'Ancien Testament*, 2 vols. (Paris, 1959).

[4] E. L. Ehrlich, "Religieuze stromingen in het Jodendom," in *Christus en Israel* 11, 2 (June 1968), pp. 9-15, previously published in *Die christlich-jüdische Arbeitsgemeinschaft in der Schweiz* (1968).

sciousness. The historic center of Jewish worship was lost with the destruction of the temple of Jerusalem,[5] and it still has not been restored with the result that the structure of Jewish worship still has something provisional about it and this encourages pluriformity. It can hardly be denied that this has created a split in Judaism, felt more acutely than ever before. The diaspora in which the Jews had to live in actual fact and which, far from being favorable to them, constituted a constant menace, saw to it that Jews of the most divergent tendencies were nevertheless thrown together in one common destiny. This was not a little encouraged by the fact that the Jews not only studied their history as an academic subject but celebrated it as salvation history in their worship.[6]

In spite of all these difficulties the answers to the questions set out below will provide some insight in the vitality of Jewish worship and frequently help the Christian pastorally toward a better understanding of his own worship.

1. *Which religious feasts are celebrated by Jews all over the world, and which only occasionally or by specific groups?*

Judaism is an attitude to life rather than a creed. In this context no Jew is totally indifferent toward any Jewish feast, and in this sense one may say that all Jews celebrate all Jewish feasts in one way or another. To bring some necessary clarity into this general assertion it is useful to distinguish between the various feasts as well as between the various ways in which modern Jews practice their common faith. Insofar as the feasts are concerned, there are the great annual feasts of the old Israel: the feast of the Unleavened Bread, the feast of Weeks and the feast of Tabernacles—three feasts with a pilgrimage—and then the Passover

[5] C. Thoma and others, *Auf den Trümmern des Tempels* (Vienna, 1968).

[6] L. Koerhuis, "De Joodse geschiedenis, een blijvende presentie van God," in *Christus en Israel* 8, 2 (April 1965), p. 31: "One of the stipulations of that law, the Torah, which helps the people to remain within the living covenant, is the liturgical celebration of God's great deeds of salvation in the history of the people."

which was eventually linked with the feast of Unleavened Bread. During the last centuries of the Old Testament several feasts were added among which three have continued to be celebrated to this day: the feast of Atonement, the *Chanukah* (the dedication of the Temple) and the *Purim*. In recent days another one has been added, the *Yom Ha'atsmuth* (Independence Day), but this has a political rather than a religious meaning.

As to the manner of celebrating, one may distinguish three main tendencies among modern Jews: the orthodox Jews, the conservative Jews and the reform movement or progressives. These are very loose categories which would be described differently in Jerusalem than, for instance, in the United States. To mark the differences in attitude toward the feasts these categories can be used as explained by Ehrlich.

The orthodox Jews cling to the religious regulations of biblical times as they were constantly explained anew by the Talmud and the medieval authorities. Although here, too, there has been some adaptation, some touching up and modernization, these changes have not affected the content but only some external forms. They celebrate all the feasts with a scrupulous ritualism. In modern Israel they prevail through a kind of privilege of the firstborn; the conservatives and the reform movement have very little influence.

The reform movement already started in the 19th century. The liturgy was reformed and abridged, and the vernacular was introduced. They also paid attention to the aesthetic shaping of the liturgy. These measures were based on a fresh interest in Jewish history and therefore affected mainly those feasts that had an historical or cultural background. The reform Jews are close to the orthodox from whom they have taken over a number of traditions without however sharing their ideological principles.

Between the orthodox and the reform movement there are the conservatives, a misnomer. Between the "conservatives" and the reform Jews there is but a difference of degree. They began in America for the preservation in America of historical Judaism. They celebrate the same feasts as the orthodox. They form a large group of Jews who are religiously interested but not orthodox and do not agree with the reformers, and this mainly from emotional motives because, according to them, the reformers deviate too far from a tradition with which they feel themselves bound up, however loosely. Among them we may count great minds such as Buber, Rosenzweig and Devinas who have made a profound study of the problems of Judaism in this modern world. They were only moderately interested in the progressive movement. All three streams, in common, view the celebration of the Jewish feasts as a collective expression of the whole Jewish community; for none of them is it a matter of individual devotion, but always the actualization of the history of the whole people with an eye on the future and never a kind of nostalgic hankering back to the past.

2. *Where do the modern Jews find support for their consciousness as a people?*

Everybody will remember how the recovery of the whole of Jerusalem was looked upon as a religious event by the Israelis. The comparison with the struggle between David and Goliath filled the atmosphere. The point here, however, was the interpretation of a religious and political event in the present time against the religious background of the Old Testament rather than a memorial celebration of the past. With the great feasts Jewish thought turns mainly to the past. On those occasions the Jew turns toward God and at the same time becomes aware of the history of his people; he lives this history in communion with other Jews and feels himself as a link in the chain of generations. The Jew is of course also aware of his responsibility for his actions as an individual, but in Judaism the community always comes first. The celebration of feasts is experienced as the expression of the heart of Judaism: God, Torah and Israel are one. The mutual aspect of the covenant, too, plays a part in these celebrations. It is not only the Jew who, in communion with his whole people, commemorates and celebrates this past, but Yahweh himself remembers this past in order to pursue the guidance of his people in the same direction. For the Jew there is continuity in Yahweh's saving deeds, based on the enduring validity of the covenant and the undiminished power of Yahweh's promises. Thus, God's creative activity in election, deliverance, covenant, Torah and in all his deeds, which make up the history of salvation, is fundamental for the present situation and directed toward a fulfillment in the future.

The events which are in this way commemorated and celebrated, powerfully reinforce the unity of the People of God throughout the centuries and together constitute the starting point, the center, the climax and the source of the existence of the Jews as the People of God. Hence, Israel's prayer and meditation constantly turns to these events in order to find there the necessary nourishment on its way to the future.[7]

3. *Are these feasts only commemorations of Yahweh's earlier deeds as narrated in what the Christians call the Old Testament?*

To commemorate and to remember is in the Jewish tradition never a mere memory but always implies a look toward the future, a promise and a making present again. Ignorance of this fact has led to the Christian prejudice about a post-biblical Judaism without history (*Geschichtslosigkeit*). The recapitulation of God's saving deeds continues to have a revolutionary effect in modern days and in traditional circles even up to the present moment. It stirs the conscious expectation that soon there will be more such deeds of Yahweh. Religious poetry which recalled the past in epic form had, at the end of antiquity and in the beginning of the Middle Ages, the effect of messianic-revolutionary pamphlets. In a secular way this aspect is still present in the State of Israel, particularly among the Zionists.[8] The memorial cele-

[7] L. Koerhuis, *art. cit.,* p. 32; B. van Iersel, "Some Biblical Roots of the Christian Sacrament," in *Concilium* 31 (1968), pp. 5-20.

[8] A. C. Ramselaar, "De dituatie van het Joodse godsdienstige leven in Israel," in *Christus en Israel* 11, 2 (June 1968), esp. p. 20, gives some examples: "On the banners displayed on Independence Day one read, 'This is the day made by Tsahal (the Israeli army) instead of the Lord' (Ps. 118); the Declaration of Independence of 1948 said, 'The State of

bration of the past, combined with an archeology which has become a national hobby, serves to inspire and strengthen the modern effort which is interwoven with the traditional messianic expectation. The pilgrimage of 300,000 pilgrims to the Wailing-Wall on the feast of the Jewish Pentecost, June 14, 1967, showed an expected revival of religious consciousness. On such occasions it is obviously difficult to distinguish between religious and national consciousness, and still harder to decide how far religious feelings are channelled in the direction of national politics. Nor is this really necessary since it is typical of the way in which the Jews celebrate their history that they commemorate a religious event not merely as a believing community but also as an ethnic group.[9] This becomes clearer still when we take a closer look at the great Jewish feasts, particularly in the way they are celebrated today. For the sake of clarity we preserve the division mentioned above: the four ancient feasts of Unleavened Bread, of Weeks, of Tabernacles and of the Passover, and the three later ones, of Atonement, *Chanukkah* and *Purim*.

(a) *The Feast of Unleavened Bread*

This feast probably goes back to the days when Israel still led a semi-nomadic existence. It is a spring festival and was the signal for the "exodus" toward new pastures. The sacrifice (without a priest and unrelated to an altar) plays an important part. In actual fact it was already blended with the feast of the Exodus, which celebrated the formation of the People as such. In today's celebration the emphasis falls indeed on this "constitution" of the People, the deliverance from slavery, while the oldest elements of

Israel will be based on the foundations of freedom, justice and peace, according to the *visions* of Israel's prophets. Trusting in the Rock of Israel, the following have signed . . . Shabbath 5th Ijar 5708—14th May, 1948. After the enthusiasm of the first years the harsh reality began to be realized. Zionism was no longer a vision. It was clear that the miracles of technology did not only occur in Israel. Inevitably the question was asked: What more has the State of Israel to offer us as Jews than independence and military power?"

[9] J. B. Agus, *The Meaning of Jewish History* (New York, 1964), Vol. II.

the spring festival where an animal was sacrificed in order to obtain the welfare of the herd have completely vanished. That is why we should link this with the *Pesach*.

(b) *The Pesach (or Passover)*

For a people that celebrates its history in its worship the moment of its birth is bound to exercise a powerful influence on this celebration. The rise of the State of Israel [10] has underlined the relevance of this feast. Less than ever before is it limited to the mere remembrance of a distant past. It is much more the religious actualization of what is happening now and a pointer to the future.

Basically the feast is dominated by the religious conviction that God delivered Israel from the slavery of Egypt, not in order to make it just a *great* nation, but a great nation that serves him. It was also the festival of the community *par excellence* which was given an extensive celebration in the religious center of the people, the temple of Jerusalem. Since the destruction of the temple in 70 A.D. it has become, above all, a family feast with a ritual adapted to domestic celebration. Jewish tradition (*Mishna Pes.* X, 5) has underlined this domestic character: "From generation to generation everyone must consider himself as having personally gone out of Egypt."

In the early Middle Ages there existed a small book which regulated the various customs in use on this feast in order to obey this instruction correctly. The Hebrew word for organization or regulation is *seder,* and hence the two evenings that precede this feast are called *seder.* The little book which provides the reading for these evenings is called the "Haggada Narrative". It contains explanations and interpretations, taken from the rich rabbinic literature, which explain the meaning of the story of the exodus to those that take part. The domestic reading of this little book is put in the context of a prescribed festival meal.

[10] B. Halphen, *The Idea of the Jewish State* (Cambridge, Mass., 1961); A. Hertzberg, *The Zionist Idea. An Historical Analysis and Reader* (New York, 1960); A. L. Sachar, *A History of the Jews* (New York, 1965, 5th ed.).

Several factors have contributed to the rise of this *Haggada*. When temple worship ceased with the destruction of the temple in the year 70, it was felt necessary to bring some order and system into the liturgy. This developed quickly under the influence of the Midrash exegesis. The families needed a small and handy manual which contained the numerous regulations for the feast of the Passover. Moreover, at the time that this *Pesachhaggada* was put together the Jews has no longer a State of their own but were subject to the Roman empire. They had lost their autonomy and needed to be delivered once again from servitude. The Passover rites stressed this urge toward freedom: they were not allowed to celebrate this feast sitting straight but in the position which only the free man was allowed to take in Rome: the reclining position on a dining couch. A similar text of the rabbinic tradition stated: "Rabbi Levi said: While slaves are accustomed to sit straight when they eat, the Jew must take the Passover meal in a reclining position in order to show that man has been redeemed from slavery" (*Jer. Pes.* X, 37b). Even the poorest in Israel must not eat otherwise than in this reclining position (b. *Pes.* X,1).

At the Passover the Jews now celebrating the exodus from Egypt identify themselves with those that actually did leave Egypt: past and present coincide.

That is why every Jew can celebrate this feast of *Pesach:* it still remains the expression of his desire for freedom and of the identity of his people. At present the orthodox will be inclined to emphasize the national elements, while the reformers and conservatives will put the emphasis rather on the religious content of this freedom and the non-political character of the Jewish community. ("We are more than merely a people.") The aspect of acutality, however, is common to both sides. This is not only caused by the narrative of the exodus but also by the fact that this feast is celebrated as a family feast. Because it is celebrated at home and not only in the synagogue, it is not merely a male occasion but women and children also take an active part in it. The *Haggada* says that the youngest member of the family must demand an explanation of the meaning of this rather formal meal. The reader of the *Haggada* is then given a chance to delve a little more deeply into all the aspects which still concern the Jewish people of today: the certainty about the covenant between God and his People and the importance of the family without which there would be neither a Jewish life nor a Jewish people. This *seder* evening exercises a very powerful appeal which no Jew can escape, regardless of what group he belongs to. At the Passover the Jew experiences his unity with the people and Jewish pluralism has here less influence than is usually assumed. This pluralism springs from other sources than the one they have all in common and which is the foundation of their unity, differences in countries of origin (America, the East, Israel, Western Europe, Portugal, etc.) and differences of a philosophical nature. Judaism does not exactly suffer under the burden of its pluralism; it is rather a sign of vitality. The Jew sees this pluralism simply as a matter of various ways of interpreting religion. Judaism has always been opposed to a dogmatization of its faith; it is rather an attitude to life which consciously accepts the Jewish tradition. And no feast is perhaps more suitable to the expression of this than the Passover. It fits in with the Jew's feelings whether he celebrates it in a kibbutz in Israel or in a liberal Jewish household in West Berlin or with reform Jews in New York or Melbourne.[11]

(c) *The Feast of Weeks*

If the feast of the Unleavened Bread reminded the Jews of Israel's nomadic existence which was later linked with the feast of deliverance and the birth of the nation, the feast of Weeks reminds them of Israel's agricultural period. It is a rustic feast, a kind of harvest festival. Later on, this feast, too, was also infused with the commemoration of an event of salvation, the covenant. It is clear that the feast of Weeks fits in with the Passover when we put the growth of the themes of these two feasts side by side:

[11] "Die geistige Gestalt des gegenwärtigen Judentums," in *Herder Korrespondenz* 22, 5 (May 1968), pp. 221-3.

a feast of nomads—a feast of peasants; a spring festival—a harvest festival; exodus—covenant; freedom—Torah; autonomy —being bound to covenant and law. This feast shows how, for the Jew, God, Torah and Israel are one. In contrast to the Passover, the feast of Weeks has no special ceremonies. Conservatives and some reform Jews have introduced the custom of inviting boys and girls to give a public pledge of their loyalty to the covenant. The orthodox commemorate at this feast the medieval and modern pogroms which often took place at this time of the Jewish year.

(d) *The Feast of Tabernacles*

From being a harvest festival with a joyful character in olden days this feast became later a joyful commemoration of the fact that Israel has a Torah. In the synagogue the scrolls of the law are carried in procession around the pulpit. This originally agricultural feast of peasants thanking God for the harvest has also been connected with an event of salvation in the Jewish tradition: the Israelites had to live in bowers in memory of the bowers in which Yahweh had made their ancestors live after the exodus from Egypt (cf. Lev. 23, 43). This connection between the bowers of the original harvest festival and the tents in which the Israelites lived in the desert may strike the critical reader as rather farfetched. It is important, however, to see that this feast, too, commemorates not only an event of the past but also the present, namely, the common destiny of the Jews on their way through history. Although the pilgrimage which was at the time of the temple combined with the celebration of this feast has disappeared, this does not diminish the relevance of the celebration. If this note of actuality is typical of the four older feasts, it is just as typical of the three younger feasts, the feasts of Atonement, the *Chanukkah* and the *Purim*.

(e) *The Day of Atonement ("Yom Kippur")*

Although *Yom Kippur* is still today one of the great solemnities of Judaism, and is even called the "day of days" in the

Mishnah, this feast of 10th Tishri (Sept.-Oct.) was unknown in the period before and immediately after the exile in the Old Testament.

If the Passover celebrates the deliverance of the Jewish people, the Day of Atonement celebrates the deliverance of the individual Jew, and while the Passover is a domestic feast, the Atonement is a feast of the synagogue. After a ritual leave-taking at home the whole family goes to the synagogue where it spends practically the whole day. The Jew sees this feast as the main pause in the Jewish year, the day when he confesses his own failures and those of his people in the certainty that a new beginning is both possible and necessary for the fulfillment of the People's mission among men. The old elaborate ritual that took place in the temple (cf. Lev. 16) has been simplified to suit the synagogue. It is also the day when the Jew who has become alienated from his people returns and does penance. The feast is really an institutionalized expression of that attitude of conversion on which the prophets so constantly insisted (cf. Jer. 18, 8; Hos. 14, 1ff.). While the ritual given in Leviticus stresses the purification of the temple from all ritual impurity, the Mishnah explains this day already as a day of ethical purity and moral regeneration. This is also the day when the Jew remembers the dead. This is not merely a moment of piety devoted to the dead but also a remembrance of those human lives which history has claimed in the course of the centuries. The shadow of the Spanish Inquisition which compelled 150,000 Jews to become Christians in the 15th century, still hovers over the *Kol Nidrei* which the cantor recites in the synagogue. The Jew experiences this feast, therefore, not only as a deliverance from his own sinfulness but also from all coercion which oppressed the Jewish community. And this, too, is not merely a matter of the past.

(f) *The "Chanukkah"*

The historical background of this feast is the military revolt of Judas the Maccabee against Antiochus, the monarch of Syria, which aimed at securing freedom of conscience for the Jews against the infiltration of Hellenism. One of Judas' first deeds after his victory was the rededication of the temple (*chanukkah* means inauguration or renewal) on 25th Kislew (Nov.-Dec., 165 B.C.—this has led some people wrongly to connect this feast with the Christian Christmas). This rededication of the temple was celebrated with elaborate solemnity and it was decided to make this an annual event (cf. 1 Mac. 4, 36-39).

Since the temple of Solomon (1 Kgs. 8, 2 and 15) and the rebuilt altar of the second temple (Ezra 3, 4) were dedicated on the feast of Tabernacles, the Chanukkah was frequently linked with this feast. Apart from the processions in the temple the ritual prescribed the waving of branches of ivy, palms and other greenery, accompanied by the singing of hymns. In the Mishnah, as in today's celebration, the Chanukkah is, above all, a feast of light. This is probably connected with the fact that at the rededication of the temple the seven-branched candlestick which had not burned for three years was rekindled. There is a legend which says that the Maccabees at the conquest found a small flask of holy oil in the temple of Jerusalem, sufficient to keep the *menorah* burning for one whole day. It burned, however, as if by miracle, for eight days. The first impression an outsider gets of this feast is that it is meant for children. They are given presents and for eight days they are given "candle-money". In spite of this custom this popular feast still means for the Jew an appeal to his conscience to protect his freedom in order to make it possible for him to live according to his convictions.

(g) *The "Purim"*

This feast, which gives one the impression of a Jewish carnival, complete with masquerades and drinking bouts, originated in the Jewish communities of the Eastern diaspora. It probably preserves the memory of a pogrom from which the Jews escaped in a way that seemed to them nothing less than miraculous. This escape is related in Esther. Haman, vizir of the Persian king Ahasuerus (Xerxes), was determined to exterminate the Jews and had fixed by lot 14th Adar (Feb.-March) for the execution of his purpose. Esther, however, and her uncle Mordecai, managed to turn the tables on Haman who himself was executed. This was joyous relief for the Jews. This story, more an historical tale than true historical fact, is read in the synagogue at the feast of *Purim*. At this reading a great deal of noise must be made when the name of Haman, the archenemy of the Jews, is first mentioned as a sign of indignation and aversion.

It is a curious feast with little religious inspiration. The name of God is scrupulously avoided in the narrative. But it expresses only too well the fate the Jews suffered in many a pogrom and persecution so that it fits in well with the feelings of the modern Jew. There are even several local celebrations of *Purim* (e.g., the Wintz *Purim* of Frankfurt) which commemorate the fact that the Jews could occasionally escape the evils designed against them. More than any other Jewish feast *Purim* is wrapped in folklore and local customs. It has also been suggested by some that it is a New Year's celebration taken over by Israel from Babylon, this mainly because of the masquerades and the drinking bouts, but also because of the lack of religious atmosphere at this feast. The fact remains that *Purim* is the most popular Jewish feast and one can hardly say that it is lacking in relevancy.

One would have to take part in the feasts described above and share the peculiar atmosphere of their prayers, hymns, rites and symbols to realize that these celebrations are not a mere remembrance but the ritual celebration of a salvation history which does not belong to the past.

4. *What part does the temple of Jerusalem play in these feasts?*

The description given above shows already that most of these feasts were originally celebrated in the central sanctuary of Israel, the temple of Jerusalem. But since this temple was the national sanctuary, situated in the national capital, and was the religious center for the people, its destiny was obviously closely tied up with the political and religious history of the kingdom. This continued till the temple was destroyed, almost four centuries after it had been built.

After the Babylonian exile a second temple was built of which Ezekiel had a vision during that exile (cf. Ezek. 40, 1—44, 9). This was looted by Antiochus Epiphanes in 169 B.C. but restored by Judas the Maccabee. This restoration is celebrated by the feast of *Chanukkah,* as mentioned above. About a century later Pompey entered the temple after his conquest of Jerusalem but showed respect and did not touch the treasure. In 20-19 B.C. Herod the Great undertook a total reconstruction of the temple which was finished in outline some ten years later, although thousands of laborers were still working at it till 64 A.D. After the conquest and destruction of Jerusalem by the Romans, no new temple has been built.[12] On the site of the earlier temple the Mohammedans built the mosque of Omar.

Just as the great feasts commemorated the events connected with the exodus from Egypt and the ark reminded the Jews of the covenant between God and his People, so the temple symbolized the election of Jerusalem and the dynasty of David, and the divine protection implied in this election.[13] The destruction of the temple was therefore obviously a turning point in the history of Jewish worship.[14] The significance of this destruction and its being succeeded by the building of a pagan temple is nevertheless often exaggerated by both Jews and Christians as if it meant the approaching end of the world or a divine confirmation of Christianity.[15] The only demonstrable result of the destruction has

[12] H. Cazelles, *Naissance de l'Eglise. Secte juive rejectée?* (Paris, 1968).

[13] For the various tendencies see the special number of *Esprit* (Sept. 1966) which provoked a number of different reactions.

[14] W. Baier, "Werden die Christen in der jüdischen Liturgie verwünscht?" in *Orientierung* 32, 5 (15 March 1968), pp. 57-8 and S. Lauer, "Christendiskriminierung im jüdischen Gebet?"; E. L. Ehrlich, "Im Haus des Judentums gibt es viele Zimmer," in *Christus en Israel* 32, 13 and 14 (15 and 31 July 1968), pp. 162 and 163.

[15] The Bar Kochba revolution of A.D. 132-5 was a much greater menace to Judaism than the destruction of the temple. That the destruction of the temple made a real break in the development of Judaism is accepted by M. Noth, *Geschichte Israels* (Berlin, 1965, 3rd ed.), pp. 13-5 and 389-400; C. Roth, *A History of the Jews* (New York, 1964, 3rd ed.), p. 111, thinks that the destruction only meant something for a particular period; it is seen as extremely important for Christianity by S. G. F.

been a more sober ritual of the Jewish feasts which now had to be adapted to a celebration at home or in a usually small synagogue. But the Jews' awareness of their identity has continued undiminished in this simplified celebration, without the temple.

The function of the temple has, however, again become actual since the end of the six-days' war in 1967. Now the Israelis have once more gained possession of the whole piece of ground where the old temple stood.[16] The orthodox Jews, who dominate the religious aspect of Jewry in Israel, have so far not made any suggestions for a rebuilding of the temple. This is hardly astonishing when we remember that Jewish worship has totally grown away from the sacrificial ritual of the temple. Even when the temple still existed the sacrificial ritual had already begun to show more spiritual features. What could one do with a new temple? To reintroduce the sacrificial liturgy would be an anachronism which would put off even the most conservative orthodox Jew. How could they recruit a new priesthood on the basis of the Levitical regulations of Scripture and the Jewish tradition? When there is a demand for a rebuilding of the temple it comes usually from nationalist quarters and a mentality which a Jewish scholar of the calibre of Werblowski qualified as a "crude nationalistic perversion of religion".[17]

To this we must add a Jewish tradition recalled recently by Chief Rabbi Nissim, which says that the third temple will be built by God himself. Although it should not be understood as a kind of dogma, it is generally believed among the Jews that the temple will be restored at the end of time. To pray for a restoration of the temple in this sense is laid down as an obligation. But this third temple which will be built at the end of time will not be built by

---

Brandon, *The Fall of Jerusalem and the Christian Church* (London, 1957, 2nd ed.), pp. 249-51, and in his *Jesus and the Zealots* (Manchester, 1967), pp. 281-2.

[16] "Der Streit um den jüdischen Gottesdienst auf dem Tempelberg," in *Herder Korrespondenz* 21 (1967), pp. 473-4. Cf. C. Thoma, "Die Zerstörung des Tempels von Jerusalem (A.D. 70) als Wende," in *Auf den Trümmern des Tempels* (Vienna/Freiburg/Basle, 1968), p. 59.

[17] *The Jerusalem Post Weekly* of August 28, 1967.

human hands but by God himself. Should this not be understood in an eschatological and spiritual sense? It is a fact that the Jews in general reject attempts such as those made by the Chief Rabbi of the Israeli army, J. Goren, to revive the memory of the old temple through the exploitation of national emotionalism. This Rabbi Goren conducted last year on 9th Aw, the anniversary of the destruction of the temple, a public religious service on the site of the temple, which had been conquered in the six-days' war. For the religious self-awareness of Judaism it will be more important that there will remain Jews who go to pray at the Wailing-Wall to discover what their mission is in this modern age.

5. *Are the Jewish celebrations mainly services of the word and is there room for improvisation?*

As we have already pointed out, at most Jewish feasts passages are read from Scripture—sometimes very lengthy—which are related to that aspect of salvation history which is celebrated. Some of these feasts, such as that of the Passover, have a ritual that is very detailed and very strict. This does not prevent most of these celebrations from leaving room for improvisation. At the *Purim* this element of improvisation occupies a large place but has a purely profane character. At the other feasts the widest margin for improvisation occurs in the domestic celebration, but it exists also in the prayer sections at the celebration in the synagogue. This holds especially for the four days which we have not mentioned yet, the four historical fast days which are related to the destruction of the temple. *Tishoh Bo'Ov*, the ninth day of Ov (July-Aug.), is the most important of these four. The three others are 10th *Teves* (Dec.-Jan.) when the Jews commemorate the beginning of the siege of Jerusalem; 17th *Tammuz* (June-July) when a breach was made in the wall of the Holy City; and 3rd *Tishri* (Sept.-Oct.) which recalls the murder of the governor of Judah by Nebuchadnezzar. This was the beginning of the Babylonian exile. The first fast day commemorates the destruction of the first temple by the Babylonians in 568 B.C. But the same day recalls the exile of the Jews from Spain in 1492 and the exile of all Jews from the Russian border provinces in 1915. Because these days are not mentioned in the Torah, the manner of celebration varies from one Jewish community to another. The reform Jews do not even celebrate these days at all because in their opinion there is no room for mourning at the destruction of the temple. For them it is the beginning of a new phase in the existence of the Jews, no doubt a tragic beginning but one which ultimately helped the Jews to be more conscious of their new mission: to be a light for all mankind.[18]

6. *Have the feasts of the present Jewish liturgy been influenced in any way by the great feasts of the Christian liturgy?*

The answer to this question is rather the reverse. This is clear from such articles as that by Barrosse in this volume about the celebration of the eucharist and that of the Passover. Some marginal influence of Christians can be traced in the celebration of the feast of *Chanukkah*. Tanenbaum refers also to the feast of Pentecost which commemorates the gift of tongues on the first Christian Whitsunday and celebrates the universalism of Christianity. A later Midrash relates something similar about the feast of Weeks. The Torah was not given for the Jews only according to this source. The tables of the law were therefore handed to Moses in the desert, a kind of no-man's-land which belongs to nobody and is the property of all. The Midrash then relates that the voice of God spread out into seventy tongues of fire because it was held that there were seventy languages in the world. In this way the Midrash tries to show the universalism of the Torah for all mankind.

The specifically ethnic element in the Jewish feasts with the consequent concern for this earth, the here and now, is too pronounced for one to expect Christian influences, since the Christian feasts are far less tied up with any people and more universal in character, and more orientated toward the beyond. The timing of the feasts may well show some correspondence but

[18] K. Thieme, *Christen und Juden* (Mainz, 1961), pp. 32-7.

this is probably due to older religious feasts. We have already pointed out that several Jewish feasts are not quite so original as may appear at first sight, and this holds even for the Passover, important though it is. Some elements of it were probably taken over by the Israelites from Egypt or still older cultures. And, of course, all these feasts are not without problems even for the Jews. This is particularly true for the reform Jews who like to take a broader view of the meaning of Judaism than the orthodox. Due to the rise of the State of Israel most feasts have, however, gained in relevance although this brought with it the danger of their being exploited for national or political purposes. There is therefore no real problem of secularization as there is with the Catholic celebration of the events of salvation.

7. *Do women and children take any part in Jewish feasts?*

Because the whole Jewish liturgy was strictly tied up with times and hours, temple-worship was of old a matter for the men, and women were dispensed. Even in the modern synagogue a special place is usually reserved for the women, although the communities of liberal Jews tend to do away with this segregation. But at the domestic celebration the women obviously play an important part. Often the woman is the main person of the feast: Deborah and Jael were praised in songs as heroines in Israel (Judges 4, 5); Athalia occupied the throne of Judah for several years (2 Kgs. 11); the prophetess Hulda was consulted by the king's ministers (2 Kgs. 22, 14ff.); and the books of Judith and Esther relate how the people were saved through the intervention of a woman.

8. *How representative of the Jewish religious celebrations is a figure like Martin Buber and his mystical approach?*

What has been said so far shows clearly that the growth of the people's identity and the possession of the land are key aspects in salvation history. Both these elements must be understood in the concrete sense, but they are open to a more spiritual interpretation. To put it in concrete terms: must God's promise of a special country for Israel necessarily be understood in the sense of a separate State? A prophetic figure like Martin Buber was far from convinced of this.[19] But prophets often are solitary beings, and Buber is no exception. One cannot say that his views are shared by Jewry at large, however important the part he played in giving new relevance to the Jewish message in our age. We do not want to enter upon a discussion of the Zionist movement or of that thorny problem whether the State of Israel should be identified with the fulfillment of God's promised land.[20] Can the present State of Israel be taken as a sign of God pursuing once again his guidance of his chosen people? Here the outsider should beware of crude alternatives. It is a fact that what has happened in recent years in Israel has made salvation history relevant again for the Jews, whether in the positive or the negative sense. It is obvious that emotions are involved and that this emotionalism is so religiously colored that it has to express itself in the celebration of the traditional feasts. Nevertheless, one can hardly ignore the fact that the "promised land" has never been a static entity which might be restored today to its original shape and greatness. In spite of all this it is possible to believe that the ties which bind the Jew to his country are not a merely historical, psychological or political matter but also a religious one. However mystical Buber may be and however close to the mystical school of the Ukraine, the *Chassidim,* he owes too much to Albert Schweitzer and Rudolf Bultmann for his attitude toward Christianity and is therefore too Western in mentality to be able to speak for the whole of Jewry. His socialist criticism of Zionism and his humanist and pacifist ideals do not endear him to the Jews of today, but there are also other reasons. In his reply to our question, Professor J. Meyer of the *Martin Buber Institut für Judaistik* at Cologne University, said that Buber's attitude to the

[19] M. Buber, "Zwei Glaubensweisen," in *Werke* I (Munich, 1963), pp. 651-82.

[20] J. J. Stamm, *Der Staat Israel und die Landverheissungen der Bibel* (Zurich/Frankfurt, 2nd ed., 1961); G. von Rad, "Verheissenes Land und Jahwes Land," in *Gesammelte Studien zum Alten Testament* (Munich, 1958).

Torah prevented him from having a clear and consistent attitude toward the Jewish feasts. A truly Jewish mystical approach to those feasts is more easily found in Abraham Isaak Kuk or in the modern theology of Joshua Heschel.

In any case, modern Judaism is such a pluralistic phenomenon that one cannot be cautious enough with generalizations. Because the boundaries between the various schools of thought are so vague it is difficult to put a label on any particular author. There simply is no dogmatic yardstick with which to measure Judaism; only the practice of the Torah determines whether one is a Jew. Their closest tie is that of the "common fate". And it is precisely this common fate which stands out most sharply in the liturgical celebrations and which gives them their relevance. The link between a practicing Jew living in one nation or another, the a-religious Zionist who only accepts the ethnic bond, and the a-religious Israeli nationalist, exists only in the mind of those Jews who identify traditional religion with national consciousness. In any case, the Jew has perhaps too many scars to see in the celebration of his history merely a liturgical commemoration. It frightens him every time when he sees that the past is not dead.

BIOGRAPHICAL NOTES

PIERRE GRELOT: Born in Paris in 1917, he was ordained in 1941. He studied in Paris at the Institut Catholique and the College of Major Studies. He earned his degree in classical Oriental languages, and is a doctor of theology. He is also professor of sacred scripture at the Institut Catholique where he also lectures on classical Oriental languages. His publications include *Introduction to the Bible* (1967) and *Man and Wife in Scripture* (1965).

THOMAS BARROSSE, C.S.C.: Born in New Orleans in 1926, he was ordained in 1950. He studied in Rome at the Gregorian and the Biblical Institute, obtaining his licentiate in theology and sacred scripture. Since 1966 he has been a member of the committee for the constitutional reform of his Order, and he has been on the editorial committee of the *Yearbook of Liturgical Studies* since 1960. His publications include *God Exists—The Biblical Record of God's Self-Revelation* (1963), and *God Speaks to Men—Understanding the Bible* (1964).

EDWARD J. KILMARTIN, S.J.: Born in the U.S.A. in 1923, he was ordained in 1954. He studied at Weston College in the U.S.A., and at the Gregorian in Rome. He earned his M.A. in philosophy and a doctorate in theology, and is professor of sacramental theology at Weston College. His publications include *The Eucharist in the Primitive Church* (1965).

LUC DEQUEKER: Born in Belgium in 1931, he was ordained in 1955. He studied at the Major Seminary of Malines, the University of Louvain, the Biblical Institute in Rome and the École Biblique in Jerusalem. He obtained his doctorate in theology and licentiates in biblical science and biblical philology. He is professor of exegesis at the Major Seminary of Malines and secretary to the National Ecumenical Commission in Belgium. He is co-author with J. Coppens of *Le Fils de l'homme et les Saints du Très-Haut en Daniel VII, dans les Apocryphes et dans le Nouveau Testament* (1961).

WILLEM ZUIDEMA: Born in Rotterdam in 1932, he is a pastor of the Free Church in Brussels. He studied at the Free University in Amsterdam, and at the Major College of Theology in Kampen, Holland. He received a doctorate in theology, and is national secretary of the Belgian Protestant Council for Judaeo-Christian Relations.

JEAN GIBLET: Born in Belgium in 1918, he was ordained in 1943. He studied at Louvain, and in Rome at the Gregorian and the Biblical Institute. After receiving licentiates in philosophy and biblical sciences, he earned his doctorate in theology. Since 1956 he has lectured on the New Testament at the University of Louvain. His publications include "Les Douze. Histoire et Théologie," in the series *Aux origines de l'Église* (1964).

ANGELO PENNA, C.R.L.: Born in Italy in 1917, he was ordained in 1940. He studied in Rome at the Angelicum and at the Biblical Institute, receiving his doctorate in biblical science and degrees in Hebrew and comparative Semitic languages. He is professor of Sacred Scripture at the Regina Mundi Academy. His publications include *San Paolo* (1951) and *La religione di Israele* (1958).

VICTOR WARNACH, O.S.B.: Born in Metz in 1909, he was ordained in 1935. He studied at the University of Bonn and at Sant Anselmo in Rome, receiving his doctorate in philosophy. He is professor of Christian philosophy at the University of Salzburg, and president of the Pontifical Institute of Philosophy at Salzburg. His published works include *Agapè. Die Liebe als Grundmotiv neutestamentlicher Theologie* (1951).

JOSEF ERNST: Born in Germany in 1926, he was ordained in 1952. He received his doctorate in theology in 1965, and since October 1968 he has been professor of New Testament theology and exegesis on the faculty of theology at Paderborn.

HEINZ SCHÜRMANN: Born in Germany in 1913, he was ordained in 1938. He received his doctorate in theology, and is currently professor of New Testament exegesis on the philosophical and theological faculty of Erfurt in Germany. His publications include *Worte des Herrn* (1966) and *Der Abendmahlsbericht Lukas 22, 7-38* (1966).

HERMAN SCHMIDT, S.J.: Born in Holland in 1912, he was ordained in 1940. He studied in Holland at the University of Nijmegen, and in Rome at the Oriental Institute, the Archeological Institute, the Institute of Sacred Music, and at the Vatican School of Paleography. He gained his licentiate in philosophy and his doctorate in theology, and he is now professor of liturgy at the Gregorian and at the Liturgical Institute of Sant Anselmo, also in Rome. In 1968 he became the director of the liturgical section of *Concilium*. His publications include *Introductio in Liturgiam Occidentalem* (1965), and *Constitutie over de H. Liturgie* (1964). He is editor of *Katholiek Archief* and a contributor to *Periodica* and *Gregorianum*.

ERNST EHRLICH: Born in Berlin in 1921, he is of the Jewish faith. He studied in Switzerland at the University of Basle, obtaining his doctorate in philosophy. He is Secretary-General of the Judaeo-Christian Friendship Committee in Switzerland, and European director of B'nai B'rith. His publications include *Kultsymbolik des Alten Testaments und des nachbiblischen Judentums* (1959) and *Der antike jüdische Statt* (1964).

MARC TANENBAUM: Born in Baltimore in 1925, he is a rabbi. He studied at the Jewish Theological Seminary of America, at the John Hopkins University in Baltimore, and at Yeshiva University in New York. He is national director of the ecumenical and interdenominational branch of the American Jewish Committee in New York. His publications include *A Guide to Jewish Traditions and Holy Days* and *Jewish-Christian Dialogue* (1966).

Subject Index to CONCILIUM (Volumes 31-40)

FIGURES IN BOLD FACE INDICATE VOLUME NUMBER
WITH PAGE REFERENCES IN LIGHT FACE

anthropological substructure of the Christian sacraments, (31) 33-50

Buddhism, the funeral rites of, (32) 156-161; Japanese, (32) 161-166

Bultmann, Rudolph, on the meaning of history, (39) 104f.

Burial, a Marxist view of, (32) 169ff.

Burial rites, African, (32) 140-143; Buddhist, (32) 156-161; Chaldean, (32) 37-44; in the Chicago experimental study, (32) 99-107; Chinese Confucianist, (32) 153-156; Gallican, (32) 46f.; Hindu, (32) 150-153; Japanese Buddhist, (32) 161-166; Jewish, (32) 167f.; Mohammedan, (32) 143-148; Mozarabic, (32) 25-35; Muslim, (32) 148f.; non-Christian, (32) 139-176; the reform of, (32) 109-116; Roman, (32) 45f.

Canonical missions, and the divine mission in history, (38) 80-87

Canon Law, proposed reforms in regard to the ministry and life of priests in, (38) 120ff.; and the sacraments in the Christian East, (38) 146-160

Castagna, Domingo, (33) 194; on whether the laity should preach today, (33) 92-98

Catholicism, the competition among ideas in, (35) 87f.

Catholic social doctrine, an analysis of recent, (35) 82-87

Cemeteries, as the final resting place of deceased Christians, (32) 53-66; the proclamation of the resurrection in our, (32) 67-74

Chadwick, Henry, (34) 181; on Anglican orders in modern Anglican theology, (34) 141-149

Chaldean funeral rite, the liturgy of the, (32) 37-44

Chanukkah, the feast of, (40) 154f.

Character, as a concrete visible element of the sacraments in relation to the Church, (31) 101-114

Charisms, as a constituent element of the Church, (33) 94; as particularizations of the universal priesthood, (34) 109-112

Chicago, the experimental funeral rite in, (32) 99-107

Chile, preaching in, (33) 147-150

China, Confucianism and burial in, (32) 153-156; the work of Père Vincent Lebbe on behalf of, (37) 113-129

Christian belief, the consequences of the hellenization of, (36) 106f.

Christian eschatology, as a message of joy, (32) 78f.

Christian groups, and their ways of life, (39) 143-162

Christian message, death and resurrection in the, (32) 7-24; the public character of contemporary society and of the, (36) 54-62

Christian sacraments, the anthropological substructure of the, (31) 33-50; the biblical roots of the, (31) 5-20

Christian worship, an analysis of, (33) 53-60

Christianity, and Marxism, (36) 102f.; the political vocation of, (36) 107f.; the revolutionary character of, (36) 101f.; the theoretical status of ideology in, (36) 85-89; the transformation of, (35) 24-30

Christians, and the concept of law, (39) 54-57; and economic life, (39) 48f.; and family life, (39) 46ff.; the final resting place of deceased, (32) 53-66; the future joy of, (39) 25ff., 99-111; the Lord's supper of the primitive, (40) 120-124; and political life, (39) 46; the spiritual offering of the life of, (33) 59f.

Christology, the historical background of politics and, (36) 72-84

Church, the administration of justice in the, (38) 134-145; the aged and the, (38) 174-177; Anglican orders and the, (34) 146-149; apostolic succession as an attribute of the whole, (34) 36-51; character as a concrete visible element of the sacraments in relation to the, (31) 101-114; charisms as a constituent element of the, (33) 94; as a communion, (37) 92-98; the consequences of social criticism for the self-understanding of the, (36) 15; the development and exposition of the apostolic word in the proclamation of the, (33) 17ff.; and the expectations of non-Christians in matters of social morality, (35) 24-45; ex-priests and the, (38) 178ff.; groups of people forgotten and neglected in the institutional, (38) 162-180; hellenistic thought as a cause of political conservatism within the, (36) 103-107; the Holy Roman Empire and the, (37) 10ff.; as the institution of free social criticism, (36) 10-18; an invitation to dialogue by the, (35) 143ff.; the Last Supper and the earliest eucharists of the, (40) 35-47; as the messianic sacrament of salvation, (31) 55-58; and modern society, (36) 82ff.; and the need to provide guidelines in social ethics, (35) 80-92; the new language of the, (36) 15f.; political conservatism and the, (36) 97-108; prophets in the present-day, (34) 60ff.; public criticism within the, (36) 16f.; recognition of the validity of Orthodox sacraments by the, (38) 155-158; the rights of the laity in the mission of the, (38) 18-24; the role of women in the functions of the, (34) 126-138; as the sacrament of salvation, (31) 53ff.; as the sacrament of the Trinity, (38) 88f.; as the sacrament of unity, (31) 58-63; as the sacrament of the world, (31) 51-66; sacramental character and the mystery of the, (31) 108-111; the sacramentality of the, (38) 1f.; the sacraments as a function of the, (38) 14f.; science and the, (37) 146-150; (38) 169-172; secular culture and the worship of the, (31) 63-66; the sick and the, (38) 172ff.; the significance of Christ's eucharistic body for the unity of the cosmos and the, (40) 106-116; social cybernetics as a permanent function of the, (35) 46-60; the social function of the, (36) 2-18; the social revolution in Latin America and the, (36) 124-135; the succession of prophets in the, (34) 52-62; the succession of teachers in the, (34) 63-73; technological culture and the, (39) 74f.; theology and social changes in the mind of the,

(35) 58f.; unmarried persons and the, (38) 177f.; the world of politics and the magisterium of the, (36) 19-39
Church government, the rights of the laity in, (38) 24-27
Church order, and the indissolubility of marriage, (38) 45-57
Clark, Francis, S.J., on Anglican orders, (31) 139-143
Collegiality, episcopal, (31) 149-164
Comfort, and suffering, (39) 93
Communal meals, of the earliest community, (40) 43-47
Communion, and the theology of the local Church, (38) 89-92
Concelebration, the practice of, (38) 70-79
Confirmation, the minister of, (38) 28-36; the proper age to receive the sacrament of, (38) 37-44
Confucianism, burial and Chinese, (32) 153-156
Congar, Yves, O.P., (31) 165; (33) 193; on the notion of major or principal sacraments, (31) 21-32; on sacramental worship and preaching, (33) 51-63
Conscience, and faith, (37) 89-92
Consecration, the transformation at the, (40) 95-102
Consoler, God as the, (39) 123-130
Constitution on the Church, on the Church as a sacrament, (38) 1, 6; on the diaconate, (38) 124-128; on the rights of the laity in the role of preaching, (38) 18f.; on the sacraments, (38) 7, 15
Constitution on the Church in the Modern World, on activity in the world, (39) 39f.; on poverty, (39) 35f.
Constitution on the Sacred Liturgy, on the Church, (38) 1, 10f.; on the rights of the laity in the celebration of the liturgy, (38) 22f.
Contemporary society, the public character of the Christian message and of, (36) 54-62
Corecco, Eugenio, (38) 182; on the bishop as head of the local Church and its discipline, (38) 88-104
Cornelius, Pope, the letter to Fabius of Antioch from, (31) 158-161; and St. Cyprian, (31) 156-162

Dulles, Avery, S.J., (34) 179; on the succession of prophets in the Church, (34) 52-62

Depuy, Bernard, O.P., (34) 180; on whether there is a dogmatic distinction between the function of priests and the function of bishops, (34) 74-86

Duss-von Werdt, Joseph, (34) 180; on what the layman can do without the priest, (34) 105-114

Easter meals, an analysis of, (40) 42f.

Ecclesial ministry, preaching and the, (33) 93f.

Economic cooperation, between neighboring countries, (35) 72f.

Economic life, the Christian view of, (39) 48f.

Ecumenism, the importance of the gradation of the sacraments for, (31) 29-32; and prophecy, (37) 99-112

Egypt, the visit of St. Francis of Assisi to, (37) 19ff.

Ehrlich, Ernst, (40) 166; on how modern Jews celebrate their history, (40) 143-163

Election, episcopal, (31) 149ff., 155-158

Empirical social study, and ethics, (35) 7-23

Empiricism, and neo-positivism, (36) 43f.

England, preaching in, (33) 151-154

Episcopal election, the basis of, (31) 149ff.; the official recognition of, (31) 155-158; the role of the faithful in, (31) 151

Episcopal college, the authority over the canonical mission of the, (38) 83f.; the missionary character of the, (38) 81

Episcopal collegiality, research notes on, (31) 149-164

Episcopal conferences, supranational, (38) 105-110

Episcopal consecration, the basis of, (31) 152-155; the official recognition of, (31) 155-158

Equipes Notre Dame, the formation and achievements of the, (39) 148ff.

Ernst, Josef, (40) 165; on the significance of Christ's eucharistic body

for the unity of Church and cosmos, (40) 106-116

Eschatological era, joy in the, (39) 21ff.

Eschatological joy, and Christ, (39) 24f.

Eschatological promises, an analysis of the, (40) 17ff.

Eschatological statement, the theological structure of an, (32) 8-11

Eschatology, and the beatitudes, (39) 38ff.; Christian, (32) 78f.; and political theology, (36) 8f.; the views of Teilhard de Chardin on, (39) 113-122

Estrangement, as purification, (39) 91ff.

Ethics, empirical social study and, (35) 7-23; and present-day politics, (36) 40-57; the relationship between faith and, (36) 94ff.; social cybernetics as a problem of, (35) 19-23

Eucharist, the earliest forms in the Church of the, (40) 35-47; the Mass and the, (40) 70-81; the orientation of the sacraments of character to the, (31) 112f.; real image and real presence in the, (40) 90-94; in St. John's gospel, (40) 60-69; St. Paul and the (40) 48-59; symbol and reality in the, (40) 82-105; the transformation of the Roman celebration of the, (40) 132-140

Evangelical inspiration, and the signs of the times, (36) 22-36

Evangelical Revival, the beginnings of the, (37) 49f.

Excommunication, the essential meaning of, (38) 7

Existential ethics, in the works of Karl Rahner, (35) 127-130

Existentialism, and personalism, (36) 41f.

Exodus, the Passover and the, (40) 27f.

Ex-priests, and the Church, (38) 178ff.

Fabius of Antioch, the letter of Pope Cornelius to, (38) 158-161

Factual, the normative power of the, (35) 15-19

Faith, and conscience, (37) 89-92; the relationship between ethics and,

Hell, the reality of, (32) 83f.

Hellenistic thought, as a cause of political conservatism within Christendom, (36) 103-107

Herder-Dorneich, Philipp, (35) 179; on how the Church can provide guidelines in social ethics, (35) 80-92

Hereafter, and joy in the biblical books, (39) 17-31

Hierarchy, sacraments and the, (38) 12ff.

Hillman, Eugene, C.S.Sp., (33) 195; on polygyny, (33) 173-192

Hindus, the funeral rites of the, (32) 150-153

Hippie movement, the significance of the, (39) 78ff.

Historical ideals, the conflict of, (36) 112ff.

Historical initiatives, the conflict of, (36) 115f.

History, the conflict of the interpretations of, (36) 120f.; the divine mission in, (38) 80-87; and revelations, (37) 85-89

Hoffmann, Karlheinz, S.J., (33) 195; on the mass media and proclamation, (33) 155-167

Holland, preaching in, (33) 136ff.

Holy Roman Empire, the Church and the, (37) 10ff.

Holy Spirit, in the gospel of St. John, (33) 11ff.

Hornef, Josef, (38) 182; on restoring the diaconate, (38) 123-132

Houtart, François, (36) 182; on the socio-political implications of Vatican Council II, (36) 85-96

Hucke, Helmut, (32) 179; on the Roman Instruction on music in the liturgy, (32) 119-136

Hughes, John Jay, (31) 166; on recent studies of the validity of Anglican orders, (31) 135-146

Huizing, Petrus, S.J., (38) 181; on the administration of justice in the Church, (38) 134-145; on the indissolubility of marriage and Church order, (38) 45-57

Human life, the integration of, (31) 33-36

Human sin, the problem of, (40) 15-19

Ideology, sociology as a critique of,

(35) 10f.; the theoretical status in Christianity of, (36) 85-89

Ignatius Loyola, St., as a prophet, (37) 27-43

Imposition of hands, apostolic succession and the chain of, (34) 87-104

Individual, the defense of the (36) 12f.; demythologization and the, (36) 4ff.

Institutionalization, religious, (36) 136-157

International cooperation, development through a program of, (35) 61-79

Inward religion, in the 18th century, (37) 47f.

Islam, the dialogue of St. Francis of Assisi with, (37) 21-25; and medieval Christendom, (37) 14-17

Italy, preaching in, (33) 121-125

Jamaa, the formation and achievements of the, (39) 152f.

Japan, Buddhism and cremation in, (32) 161-166

Javierre, Antonio, S.D.B., (33) 179; on the traditional teaching on apostolic succession, (34) 16-27

Jesus Christ, the apostles and the risen, (34) 13; as the blessed experience, (39) 40-43; the claim to messiahship of, (36) 97ff.; the death of, (32) 14f,, 18-21; and eschatological joy, (39) 24f.; participation in the life of, (39) 34-37; as a political messiah, (36) 97-100; as reconciliation personified, (33) 88; the relationship between the apostolic proclamation and, (33) 10f.; the relationship of our death and resurrection to that of, (32) 18-21; the revelation in St. Paul of, (33) 11; the resurrection of, (32) 15-21; sacramental character and participation in the priesthood of, (31) 105-108; the significance for the unity of Church and cosmos of the eucharistic body of, (40) 106-116; the witness of St. Luke to, (33) 13; as the Word of God, (32) 9f.; the words and actions at the Last Supper of, (40) 119-131

Jews, the burial rites of the, (32) 167f.; and the celebration of their history, (40) 143-163; the Passover ritual of the, (40) 32ff.; the

International Publishers of CONCILIUM

ENGLISH EDITION
Paulist Press
Glen Rock, N. J., U.S.A.
Burns & Oates Ltd.
25 Ashley Place
London, S.W.1
DUTCH EDITION
Uitgeverij Paul Brand, N. V.
Hilversum, Netherlands
FRENCH EDITION
Maison Mame
Tours/Paris, France
JAPANESE EDITION (PARTIAL)
Nansôsha
Tokyo, Japan

GERMAN EDITION
Verlagsanstalt Benziger & Co., A.G.
Einsiedeln, Switzerland
Matthias Grunewald-Verlag
Mainz, W. Germany
SPANISH EDITION
Ediciones Guadarrama
Madrid, Spain
PORTUGUESE EDITION
Livraria Morais Editora, Ltda.
Lisbon, Portugal
ITALIAN EDITION
Editrice Queriniana
Brescia, Italy